ULTIMATE WIFE

Discovering How Every Woman Can Be a Dream Wife

by
Richmond Donkor

Copyright © 2014 by Richmond Donkor

All rights reserved. No part of this book may be reproduced, stored in a retrieval system, or transmitted in any form or by any means, electronic, mechanical, photocopying, recording, scanning, or otherwise, without the prior written permission of the publisher.

Edited by Paladin Proofreading (www.paladinproofreading.com)

Scripture references are taken from the following versions of the Bible (accessed from *BibleGateway.com*):

Scripture quotations marked (ASV) are taken from the American Standard Version Bible, Copyright © 1901.

Scripture quotations marked (CEB) are taken from the Common English Bible®, CEB® Copyright © 2010, 2011 by Common English Bible.™ Used by permission. All rights reserved worldwide. The "CEB" and "Common English Bible" trademarks are registered in the United States Patent and Trademark Office by Common English Bible. Use of either trademark requires the permission of Common English Bible.

Scripture quotations marked (CEV) are taken from the Contemporary English Version, Copyright © 1991, 1992, 1995 by American Bible Society. Used by permission.

Scripture quotations marked (ESV) are taken from The Holy Bible, English Standard Version (ESV), copyright © 2001 by Crossway Bibles, a publishing ministry of Good News Publishers. Used by permission. All rights reserved.

The Holman Christian Standard Bible®, Copyright © 1999, 2000, 2002, 2003, 2009 by Holman Bible Publishers. Used by permission. Holman Christian Standard Bible®, Holman CSB®, and HCSB® are federally registered trademarks of

Holman Bible Publishers.

Scripture quotations marked (KJV) are taken from the King James Bible.

Scripture quotations marked (NASB) are taken from the New American Standard Bible®, Copyright © 1960, 1962, 1963, 1968, 1971, 1972, 1973, 1975, 1977, 1995 by The Lockman Foundation. Used by permission. (www.Lockman.org)

Scripture quotations marked (NIV) are taken from the Holy Bible, New International Version. Copyright © 1973, 1978, 1984 by International Bible Society. Used by permission of International Bible Society.

Scripture quotations marked (NKJV) are taken from the New King James Version®. Copyright © 1982 by Thomas Nelson, Inc. Used by permission. All rights reserved.

Scripture quotations marked (NLT) are taken from the Holy Bible, New Living Translation, copyright © 1996. Used by permission of Tyndale House Publishers, Inc., Wheaton, Illinois 60189. All rights reserved.

Other scriptures were taken from the following versions of the Bible (accessed from *BibleHub*) as noted in the text:
The Original Aramaic New Testament in Plain English with Psalms and Proverbs, Copyright © 2007; 8th ed. Copyright © 2013. All rights reserved.

The Holy Bible: International Standard Version® Release 2.1, Copyright © 1996-2012 by The ISV Foundation. All rights reserved internationally.

All emphasis in Scripture quotations added unless otherwise noted.

TABLE OF CONTENTS

INTRODUCTION
It's Not Easy — 1

CHAPTER ONE
She is God-Fearing — 17

CHAPTER TWO
She Loves Unconditionally — 35

CHAPTER THREE
She Uses Godly Speech — 45

CHAPTER FOUR
She is Industrious — 57

CHAPTER FIVE
She Dresses Modestly — 71

CHAPTER SIX
She Loves Children — 82

CHAPTER SEVEN
She is Mature of Mind — 94

CHAPTER EIGHT
She is Humble — 103

CONCLUSION
The Ultimate Wife, a Woman of Virtue — 117

INTRODUCTION

It's Not Easy

A friend of mine introduced me to a song, by Lucky Dube, called "It's Not Easy." The lyrics took me aback with their insight into a root cause of the trouble that afflicts many marriage—lack of advance knowledge about the other person's true character.

This song contrasts the excitement that generally accompanies a young couple's decision to get married with the cautionary advice of a concerned parent. When two people decide to marry, most friends and relatives express excitement for that decision. Others, often including spiritual mentors like parents and pastors, may also harbor reservations about the readiness of the couple or the suitability of the match. When people are in love, however, they tend to become blind to each other's faults or incompatibilities until vows are already

THE ULTIMATE WIFE

exchanged.

The lyrics of "It's Not Easy" speak to the dishearteningly common consequences of such blindness:

> I remember the day I called mama on the telephone
> I told her mama I'm getting married, I could hear her voice
> On the other side of the telephone, she was smiling
> And she asked me a question that I proudly answered
> *She said, Son did you take time to know her?*
> I said mama she's the best but today it hurts me so
> To go back to mama and say mama I'm getting divorced
> Oh I'm getting divorced
> This choice I made didn't work out
> The way I thought it would...
> I remember in church, when the preacher read the scriptures
> You looked so beautiful and innocent
> I did not know that behind that beauty
> Lies the true colours that will destroy me in

THE ULTIMATE WIFE

the near future...
Oh Lord I'm hurting now...

(by Lucky Philip Dube, Warner/Chappell Music, from MetroLyrics, *emphasis added)*

The question that the speaker's mother asks him on the telephone—"Son did you take time to know her?"—is not an unusual question for a mother to ask her son when he finds a women he wants to marry. More knowledge early in a relationship can avoid conflict, heartache, and grief later on.

A good mother wants her son to find a wife who possesses qualities similar to her own. Like the speaker in the song, men reply with full assurance and confidence in our choice. However, in most cases, they have no idea what they are getting into.

Mothers want to protect not only their sons but also the women involved, for a mother tends to feel partly responsible whenever unhappiness or divorce afflicts her child's marriage. A divorce hurts everyone, including the families of both husband and wife. In such cases, blame is cast about liberally; but in all fairness, a man must reconsider the question: "Did you take time to know her?"

People often ask me why divorce has become

THE ULTIMATE WIFE

rampant in our society. Although people decide to end their marriages for many different reasons, a fundamental cause of divorce is that we don't take time to know each other before we get married. Getting to know another person is a profound and complex process, which we will explore in this book. For you to know your potential spouse adequately, you must plan carefully and consider many different factors.

Most men desire to marry and have children someday. Others shy from marriage because of the process and the preparation involved. Proper preparation, however, leads to proper performance. Preparation is crucial to everything we do in life, and most relationships that suffer inordinately do so because of a poorly laid foundation. Most of the preparation that precedes marriages nowadays concerns the wedding and other ephemeral matters, which are unrelated to the growth and maintenance of a healthy, lasting relationship.

Men and women who marry usually love each other deeply, but that love too often transforms into anger and frustration, which leads in turn to separation and divorce. In such cases, something in the relationship was amiss—some problem that ought to have been prevented or addressed in order to establish a happy home.

THE ULTIMATE WIFE

Marriage requires a man to find a woman who is fit to become a proper wife, both in general and for him in particular. He must consider and contemplate his choice carefully. Finding a good wife proves overly challenging for many men, who complain that they can't find a woman who truly understands them. Oftentimes, men fail to distinguish between a pleasant woman and a proper wife. Moreover, no amount of outward beauty can make someone a good wife, nor can any amount of money buy such a wife. Finding the right partner requires the grace of God.

Having a family is important; as God saw from the beginning, mankind needs companionship. As Genesis 2:18 recounts, "Then the LORD God said, 'It is not good that the man should be alone; I will make him a helper fit for him" (ESV). The word "alone" carries the idea of being isolated, removed from the company of others and separate from any larger whole. Therefore, getting married is a serious matter for your spiritual health and the wellbeing of your soul.

Marriage Isn't for Everyone

Lest anyone who is single should get the wrong idea, however, realize that God's will is not for every person to be married. Jesus had this to say about marriage:

THE ULTIMATE WIFE

> But He said to them, "All cannot accept this saying, but only *those* to whom it has been given: **12** For there are eunuchs who were born thus from *their* mother's womb, and there are eunuchs who were made eunuchs by men, and there are eunuchs who have made themselves eunuchs for the kingdom of heaven's sake. He who is able to accept *it*, let him accept *it*."
> (Matthew 19:11-12 NKJV, emphasis in original)

In this passage, Jesus clarifies that marriage is an option, not mandatory. Regardless of the comments that friends or family members may make about your love life, you can choose to marry or choose to remain single. In God's eyes, marriage is best for some people; celibacy is best for others. Apostle Paul expressed this same idea when he said, "For I wish that all men were even as I myself. But each one has his own gift from God, one in this manner and another in that" (1 Corinthians 7:7 NKJV).

God works His plans through people in all manner of circumstances, and sometimes He determines that He can better use a person when he or she remains single. Paul explained to the Corinthians why this is so:

> But I want you to be without care. He who is

THE ULTIMATE WIFE

unmarried cares for the things of the Lord—how he may please the Lord. **33** But he who is married cares about the things of the world—how he may please *his* wife.
(1 Corinthians 7:32-33, NKJV, emphasis in original)

Therefore, instead of obsessing over your difficulties in attracting a mate, or becoming upset with the Lord as a result, perhaps the correct response would be to realize that God might have a better plan for your life.

Marriage with Purpose

If God leads you down the path of marriage, however, then you must approach the matter in all seriousness. Finding and choosing the person who will complete your life, and joining that person in holy matrimony, is no trifling affair; it requires preparation and direction. As mentioned already, God Himself knew from the start that most men need a woman to be their helper (Genesis 2:18).

The word "helper" does not indicate a slave, although some men treat their wives as such. A wife, as a helper, is not supposed to be the property or abject servant of her husband but, rather, is meant to assist him in completing particular tasks or otherwise fulfilling his

THE ULTIMATE WIFE

purpose. When referring to a spouse, "helper" speaks to the idea of one who enables and completes another. When God observed the condition of the first man He created, He decided to make Adam a helper—someone who would be suitable and fit for him, specifically.

In other words, God wanted Adam to have someone who would complete him, filling a void in Adam's soul and making up for his deficiencies. This companion would enable Adam to live the life that God meant for him to lead, including for purposes of having children (Genesis 1:28). God was serious about human community; and by creating Eve for Adam, he provided both with companionship and the means to build a family.

Therefore, men, you must not marry a woman thinking to make her your servant. God created females in order to provide men not with slaves but with human friendship in the most profound sense.

It is always a joyful experience to meet someone you love for the first time, and Adam was no exception when he first saw Eve. Today people would call his reaction "love at first sight," which is widely regarded as a fanciful notion. To some extent, however, romantic love often begins with an emotional attraction or connection that we cannot always articulate in the moment. When Adam saw Eve, he recognized their

THE ULTIMATE WIFE

sameness and knew that they were intended for one another, and this gladdened him:

Then the LORD God made a woman from the rib he had taken out of the man, and he brought her to the man.

> **23** The man said,
> "This is now bone of my bones
> and flesh of my flesh;
> she shall be called 'woman,'
> for she was taken out of man.
> (Genesis 2:22-23 NIV)

God directly created and located a wife for Adam; He did all of the work. Men today still need God to help us make the right choice in a spouse, but we also have a larger part to play in the process than Adam did. When it comes to choosing a life partner, you need to start by asking yourself why, exactly, you want to get married.

- Is it because you are getting older, so you think you have to get married?
- Is it because of pressure from your family?
- Is it because you want to have children?
- Is it because you think she is the most beautiful

THE ULTIMATE WIFE

woman you have ever met?
- Is it because you need somebody to wash your clothes and cook for you?
- Is it because the woman has helped you, so you want to marry her out of gratitude or as a kindness?
- Is it because you have gotten her pregnant, so you want to marry her to avoid gossip?
- Is it because you can't control yourself sexually?

The last reason may not serve as an especially strong foundation for a marriage in and of itself, yet it is a legitimate biblical rationale for marriage as an institution. In the words of Paul, "But since sexual immorality is occurring, each man should have sexual relations with his own wife, and each woman with her own husband" (1 Corinthians 7:2 NIV).

You need to identify one or more clear reasons why you want to get married because this will help you to achieve your goals in starting a family. If you marry for the wrong reason, you will experience the consequences down the road. You must also communicate your motivations to your potential spouse in order to ensure that he or she has the same vision or, at least, is willing to accept your goals in marriage. Too often, men and women deceive each other on this subject, which

THE ULTIMATE WIFE

becomes a problem when they eventually realize that their marriage was built on lies. Do not be so afraid to lose each other that you withhold the truth about your aims, intentions, and desires during the courtship phase of your relationship.

Most marriages fail, whether or not they end in divorce, because most men don't establish a long-term goal for the relationship. For example, if you choose to marry a woman because you can't control your sexual life, then your marriage will collapse when the time comes that your wife can no longer fulfill you in that respect. If you choose a spouse on the basis of wanting to have babies but children are not forthcoming, then discontent and divorce become likely.

If you consider the reason why God created Eve for Adam, you can see that it has lasting value. To have a helper, "completer" or complement, and companion for life is priceless; its worth never fades until death takes one or both of you to your eternal home. If you choose a woman for most of the reasons listed above, your marriage will likely falter. However, if you desire a spouse because you need a true friend to complete you and accompany you through life, then you will choose wisely and your love will endure.

Marriage as Commitment

THE ULTIMATE WIFE

As a man busily and seriously searches for a suitable wife, he should also consider how to be an excellent man and husband for his future spouse—which may in turn provide an opening for the right woman to enter his life.

All of the characteristics of the ultimate wife that we will discuss in this book also describe, at least in a general sense, the ultimate husband. Whatever you expect of your wife, you must be prepared to do as well. Jesus taught the crucial importance of the commandment "Do to others as you would have them do to you" (Luke 6:31 NIV); marriage is no exception to this principle. Are you prepared to love your wife with the love of Christ?

If you show true, godly love to your wife and care for her, she will do the same for you; but if you hold yourself and your spouse to different standards, neither of you will be happy. Therefore, you must understand the gravity of marriage and be prepared to commit wholly to your relationship with your wife. If you can do this, then God will bless your marriage and your decision to marry will prove one of the best choices you ever make in life. As the Bible says, "The man who finds a wife finds a treasure, and he receives favor from the LORD" (Proverbs 18:22 NLT).

This is not to say that either marriage or the search

THE ULTIMATE WIFE

for your ultimate wife will be without difficulty or sacrifice. To create Eve, God performed surgery on Adam, opened him up, and took out a rib. Like surgery, finding a mate often involves pain; and even after you have secured your perfect mate and exchanged vows, painful times will still ensue. However, you must learn to trust the Lord during the difficult seasons and remember your commitments to your spouse.

Entering into a marriage is like starting a lifelong journey. To successfully face challenges, reach your intended destinations, and enjoy the many other experiences that you will share along the way, you need spiritual, emotional, psychological, physical, and material preparation. Marriage is not something to be undertaken likely—or to quit when the way becomes difficult. Jesus said, quoting passages from Genesis:

> But from the beginning of the creation, God 'made them male and female.' **7** 'For this reason a man shall leave his father and mother and be joined to his wife, **8** and the two shall become one flesh'; so then they are no longer two, but one flesh. **9** Therefore what God has joined together, let not man separate.
> (Mark 10:6-9 NKJV)

THE ULTIMATE WIFE

Man is to *leave* his parents and *join* himself to his wife. This is a two-step process that many couples would do well to consider.

To leave means to place every other relationship and commitment –excluding, of course, your relationship with God—at a lower priority than your marital relationship. Your wife is truly to be your best friend. Leaving your parents, or your life and order of priorities before marriage, means that every activity outside of the marital relationship must take a backseat. This includes your career and business, sports and hobbies, your social life, and even church work. Outside of your walk with God, no other relationship or activity is as important as your spouse! As important as your job, friends, or relatives may be, your wife is always to be your top priority in life.

To join to someone means to adhere or stick to that person, tying yourself tightly to him or her by some strong bond. Joining yourself to your wife isn't an instant process or a one-time act; rather, it is a lifelong pursuit. It begins at the marriage altar and continues to the deathbed. It requires absolute, total commitment.

"Commitment" is an overused but undervalued word in our modern society, especially in the arena of marriage. The modern mindset says, "Well, we'll try it for a while, and if it doesn't work, I'll just find someone

THE ULTIMATE WIFE

new." That is a far cry from what God intended in the beginning! The 1611 King James Bible describes marriage thus: "Therefore shall a man leave his father and his mother, and shall cleave unto his wife: and they shall be one flesh" (Genesis 2:24 KJV).

Cleaving to your wife is no passive endeavor, and it goes beyond your physical union as "one flesh." It doesn't simply happen but, rather, comes about as the result of prolonged effort. The New Testament word for "join" means to stick like glue; the two elements become one, unable to be separated without damaging both ("kollaó," Strong's Concordance). If we truly believe that two people are joined in body and spirit when they are married, then we must also believe that severing their union is a grave and dangerous matter. Any marriage is therefore worth whatever effort is necessary to revive and sustain it!

Such an enormous commitment requires more than a day's or a week's contemplation, and both you and the woman concerned deserve more than an impulsive decision. Sometimes a man will rush to marry a particular woman because he fears that someone will take that woman from him. However, you must trust in God's timing and providence, and your relationship will reap blessings from time spent in thoughtful and prayerful preparation beforehand.

THE ULTIMATE WIFE

When I ask men to describe their dream wife or the ultimate wife, the answers I receive always shock me. Most guys whom I ask about their dream wife care most about the physical appearance of their future spouse, so their criteria start with beauty. Of secondary concern is having a kind and caring wife. Even the latter, however, does not in itself have everlasting value in a healthy relationship. No wonder the divorce rate is so high these days!

The following chapters focus on a range of criteria that are vitally important for a man to consider when he is praying and preparing for his future wife. Women, you will note that any woman is capable of fulfilling the criteria of a good wife. Whether you are married yet or not, this book will help women to understand how to be good wives—and men to be good husbands. Husbands and wives alike should also pray for each other to be good spouses. Of course, if you are currently unmarried, this book will better prepare and enable you to find the ultimate wife—your dream wife.

CHAPTER ONE

She is God-Fearing

Chapter 31 of the book of Proverbs contains motherly advice (Proverbs 31:10-31) for young men. The chapter is introduced as advice that "King Lemuel of Massa" received from his mother (Proverbs 31:1), "Lemuel" is widely believed to be King Solomon, the traditionally recognized author of Proverbs. Queen Bathsheba offered her wisdom to her son, Solomon, who became king. He took the advice seriously, which is why he included it in this book of wise sayings, which reads somewhat like a diary.

As a king, Solomon could choose any lady he liked. However, his mother was concerned about her son's security and happiness in his marriage. Therefore, she told her son to consider some important characteristics in searching for a wife.

THE ULTIMATE WIFE

The queen spoke from a mother's point of view because you can only offer counsel on matters about which you are knowledgeable. Listening with humility to the advice of a mother or other mentor could help you to make a wise choice regarding one of the most crucial decisions that you will ever make. Who better to give such advice than someone who herself is a good spouse, and who has cared deeply for you all your life?

When it comes to choosing a wife, most men have confused, misguided, or unclear priorities. In Proverbs 31, the queen warns her son not to be a womanizer but to choose one woman, a virtuous woman, and settle down with her. This is especially important for a king or other leader—such as a public official or a pastor—because the character of a leader's wife affects his decision-making and, thereby, the many people for whom he is responsible. This is why Proverbs 31:3 advises, "Do not give your strength to women, your ways to those who destroy kings" (ESV). However, the basic principle holds true for every man, who is head of his household: the character of your wife has a direct and profound influence on your children and a less direct, but no less real, effect on every other person in your life.

Since Bathsheba's son was a king, or would become a king, he had thousands of women from whom to

THE ULTIMATE WIFE

choose. He knew many women and had the power to make nearly any of them his, but he was perhaps struggling to choose one who would be an excellent wife and queen to stand by his side. As the old adage goes, behind every successful man, there is a woman; and, likewise, the downfall of a man is oftentimes also a woman. A good wife will help you to fulfill your purposes and achieve the goals that you have for your family. You need a *virtuous* woman who can assist you and be your companion in life.

A Virtuous Wife

Proverbs 31:10 asks, "Who can find a virtuous wife? For her worth *is* far above rubies" (NKJV, emphasis in original). Queen Bathsheba wanted her son to marry a virtuous wife. The word "virtuous" refers to strength, which in ancient times, when describing a man, often suggested physical or military strength and prowess in battle. A woman's virtue was frequently thought to reside in her physical beauty or, in more recent times, in her virginity. Here, however, "virtuous" refers to a person who is strong in character—that is, who possesses integrity.

Such a woman is more valuable than any worldly wealth. Like every good thing, a virtuous woman is hard to find; but she is also priceless, never diminishing in

THE ULTIMATE WIFE

value or appeal. A virtuous woman understands, appreciates, and supports her husband if he does not cast her aside, and she is willing to accompany him for the rest of their lives.

God Himself instituted marriage when He created Eve for Adam. Since God initiated marriage, it only makes sense that your first consideration in searching for your dream wife is to find a woman who fears God; for fear of God is "the beginning of knowledge" and wisdom, necessary for virtuous conduct (Proverbs 1:7).

Unfortunately, men are usually attracted to women primarily on the basis of appearance. All too many men truly believe in the importance of marrying a beautiful woman. They fail to realize what the queen told her son: "Charm can be deceiving, and beauty fades away, but a woman who honors the LORD deserves to be praised" (Proverbs 31:30 CEV). Bathsheba, who was herself a lovely woman (2 Samuel 11:2), acknowledged that females can exhibit physical beauty and pleasant, attractive manners, yet she emphasized that such appeal cannot be trusted; it does not last. Appearances deceive, which is why most people do, in fact, judge a book by its cover.

We don't normally think first about the inner beauty of a woman. God, however, always peers into the hearts of human being, as He made clear to Samuel when

THE ULTIMATE WIFE

guiding the prophet to choose the first king for His people: "But the LORD said to Samuel, 'Do not look on his appearance or on the height of his stature, because I have rejected him. For the LORD sees not as man sees: man looks on the outward appearance, but the LORD looks on the heart'" (1 Samuel 16:7 ESV).

The outward appeal of a woman is not unimportant. After all, a man should find his wife attractive. However, you should pray above all for a wife who fears and honors God. In this regard, it is vital to recognize that a God-fearing woman is not necessarily the same as a religious or churchgoing woman. A religious woman may know the truth and go through the motions of faith, but she doesn't truly live in accordance with the principles of faith or otherwise practice, from the heart, what she knows intellectually. Meanwhile, the churchgoing woman attends church to show off new outfits or to see friends and family, but she is there for her social life, not her spiritual life. A God-fearing woman believes and practices on a daily basis what the Bible says, and her example encourages others to come to Christ.

The primary, distinguishing characteristic of a God-fearing woman is sincere faith. Sincerity means that her belief is genuine. By contrast, it is possible to have a phony, hypocritical form of faith in which religion or

THE ULTIMATE WIFE

spirituality is only a mask to be worn in front of church members or in the public eye but set aside in the course of a person's daily life and inner life.

Moreover, it is of utmost importance to find a spouse who shares the same faith as you. Nowadays, the idea that religion doesn't matter is a commonplace. While this is accurate in the sense that particular religious doctrines and denominational differences don't reflect the vital matter of a relationship with God, faith does matter—more than anything else—when it comes to choosing a wife. Both husband and wife should be sincere believers in our one true God and our Lord Jesus Christ. If you are believer yet you marry an unbeliever, then you will struggle in your marital relationship, and your children will suffer. Paul explained the underlying problem to the Corinthians:

> Don't be tied up as equal partners with people who don't believe. What does righteousness share with that which is outside the Law? What relationship does light have with darkness? **15** What harmony does Christ have with Satan? What does a believer have in common with someone who doesn't believe? **16** What agreement can there be between God's temple and idols? Because we are the temple of the

THE ULTIMATE WIFE

living God. Just as God said, *I live with them, and I will move among them. I will be their God, and they will be my people.* **17** Therefore, *come out from among them and be separated, says the Lord. Don't touch what is unclean. Then I will welcome you.*
(2 Corinthians 6:14-17 CEB, emphasis in original)

The New International Version translates the beginning of this passage, "Do not be yoked together with unbelievers" (2 Corinthians 6:14 NIV). The yoke of which Paul speaks is no egg yolk but an allusion to Deuteronomy 22:10, which says, "Do not plow with an ox and a donkey yoked together" (NIV).

The image of the yoke used by Paul here isn't familiar to most people unless they know about ancient farming practices. We don't see yoked oxen every day; but Paul's original audience grasped the significance of the image readily. God instructed the Israelites not to plow with an ox and donkey yoked together because this unequal yoking would be harmful to the animals. The donkey would be dragged along by the much larger and stronger ox, and the independent-minded donkey might decide to pause or move in a different direction while the ox continues plowing forward. Nor would such a pairing be fair or safe for the ox, which would be

THE ULTIMATE WIFE

strained and exhausted by the added labor. Clearly, it would not be right or sensible for these animals to "be tied up as equal partners."

Paul's counsel extends beyond best farming practices, of course; he is warning believers about the danger of "yoking" two people who are traveling in different directions spiritually. Being unequally yoked in any partnership is a bad idea because it's unfair to both partners. The goal of marriage is union as one flesh, so marriage certainly yokes people together. If the husband and wife don't share a common faith, however, both of them lose. Time will reveal major differences regarding how they use their time and spend their money, which leads to bitter conflict. An unbeliever, including an adherent to a different faith, will not respond the same way a believer does to challenging circumstances. Even if a Christian husband and non-Christian wife both claim to believe and trust in God, they do not understand God the same way and cannot truly pray together; the husband's God is not the wife's god. The metaphor of the yoke illustrates effectively why marrying someone with a different faith makes for a difficult, and in some ways impossible, relationship.

Humans were created to worship and serve God. Dividing our loyalty to share our most intimate relationship with a person who doesn't believe keeps us

THE ULTIMATE WIFE

from doing what God has prepared us to do. Ask yourself: Why would I want to marry someone who would not love and enthusiastically participate in the relationship that is most important to me? With such disparity, the ability of the two people to become one would be severely damaged. Don't subject yourself to a marriage, or business partnership, or other relationship in which you'll be forced to dilute your commitment to Christ. Being single would be far better than being in a relationship that is only half of what it's supposed to be.

Solomon's Idolatrous Wives

Queen Bathsheba's son, King Solomon, offers a perfect example of this principle. Although Solomon was one of the wisest rulers who ever lived, he did not choose wisely, in accordance with his mother's advice, when it came to marriage. Instead, he took unbelieving wives who turned his heart away from God:

> Now King Solomon loved many foreign women, along with the daughter of Pharaoh: Moabite, Ammonite, Edomite, Sidonian, and Hittite women, **2** from the nations concerning which the LORD had said to the people of Israel, "You shall not enter into marriage with them, neither shall they with you, for surely they

THE ULTIMATE WIFE

will turn away your heart after their gods." Solomon clung to these in love. **3** He had 700 wives, who were princesses, and 300 concubines. And his wives turned away his heart. **4** For when Solomon was old his wives turned away his heart after other gods, and his heart was not wholly true to the LORD his God, as was the heart of David his father. **5** For Solomon went after Ashtoreth the goddess of the Sidonians, and after Milcom the abomination of the Ammonites. **6** So Solomon did what was evil in the sight of the LORD and did not wholly follow the LORD, as David his father had done. **7** Then Solomon built a high place for Chemosh the abomination of Moab, and for Molech the abomination of the Ammonites, on the mountain east of Jerusalem. **8** And so he did for all his foreign wives, who made offerings and sacrificed to their gods.

9 And the LORD was angry with Solomon, because his heart had turned away from the LORD, the God of Israel, who had appeared to him twice **10** and had commanded him concerning this thing, that he should not go after other gods. But he did not keep what the LORD commanded. **11** Therefore the LORD said

THE ULTIMATE WIFE

to Solomon, "Since this has been your practice and you have not kept my covenant and my statutes that I have commanded you, I will surely tear the kingdom from you and will give it to your servant. **12** Yet for the sake of David your father I will not do it in your days, but I will tear it out of the hand of your son. **13** However, I will not tear away all the kingdom, but I will give one tribe to your son, for the sake of David my servant and for the sake of Jerusalem that I have chosen.
(1 Kings 11:1-13 ESV)

Some believers think that they are smart or wise enough to bring an unbelieving spouse to faith, but even Solomon was not wise enough to accomplish that. Faith ultimately comes from God, not people; and as Solomon's case makes clear, He does not want us to wed ourselves to unbelievers. Doing so brings ruin to your life and to your children.

If you want God to be the foundation of your marriage, you must choose someone who fears and honor Him. If you hold different beliefs, you can't move in the same direction in life. As God observed through the prophet Amos, "Can two people walk together without agreeing on the direction?" (Amos 3:3

THE ULTIMATE WIFE

NLT). The devil blinds the eyes of unbelievers so that they see only what is material or false, and this leads them down unsafe paths. If you join yourself to such a person, then not only your marriage but also you and your family are on a road to destruction.

If you still think that your future wife's faith does not matter, consider the words of Paul, who wrote, "The god of this age has blinded the minds of those who don't have faith so they couldn't see the light of the gospel that reveals Christ's glory. Christ is the image of God" (2 Corinthians 4:4 CEB). Unbelievers walk in darkness, and no amount of determination on your part can help them to see the light.

The wife of Abraham's nephew Lot was not a believer. As a result, when the Lord directed Lot and his family to flee Sodom and Gomorrah, her heart remained with the house and material possessions that she left behind:

> With the coming of dawn, the angels urged Lot, saying, "Hurry! Take your wife and your two daughters who are here, or you will be swept away when the city is punished."
>
> **16** When he hesitated, the men grasped his hand and the hands of his wife and of his two daughters and led them safely out of the city,

THE ULTIMATE WIFE

for the LORD was merciful to them. **17** As soon as they had brought them out, one of them said, "Flee for your lives! Don't look back, and don't stop anywhere in the plain! Flee to the mountains or you will be swept away!"

18 But Lot said to them, "No, my lords, please! **19** Your servant has found favor in your eyes, and you have shown great kindness to me in sparing my life. But I can't flee to the mountains; this disaster will overtake me, and I'll die. **20** Look, here is a town near enough to run to, and it is small. Let me flee to it—it is very small, isn't it? Then my life will be spared."

21 He said to him, "Very well, I will grant this request too; I will not overthrow the town you speak of. **22** But flee there quickly, because I cannot do anything until you reach it." (That is why the town was called Zoar.)

23 By the time Lot reached Zoar, the sun had risen over the land. **24** Then the LORD rained down burning sulfur on Sodom and Gomorrah—from the LORD out of the heavens. **25** Thus he overthrew those cities and the entire plain, destroying all those living in the cities—and also the vegetation in the land. **26** *But Lot's wife looked back, and she became a pillar*

THE ULTIMATE WIFE

of salt. (Genesis 19:15-26 NIV)

Lot's wife could not help but look backward, toward death, rather than forward to life; and so she perished.

Samson's Marriage to a Philistine

The Israelite champion Samson never succeeded in his relationships with women because, like Lot, he did not choose a woman who feared God. When he tried to take an unbelieving wife, the marriage didn't last long:

> Samson went down to Timnah, and at Timnah he saw one of the daughters of the Philistines. **2** Then he came up and told his father and mother, "I saw one of the daughters of the Philistines at Timnah. Now get her for me as my wife." **3** But his father and mother said to him, "Is there not a woman among the daughters of your relatives, or among all our people, that you must go to take a wife from the uncircumcised Philistines?" But Samson said to his father, "Get her for me, for she is right in my eyes."
> **4** His father and mother did not know that it was from the LORD, for he was seeking an

THE ULTIMATE WIFE

opportunity against the Philistines. At that time the Philistines ruled over Israel.
(Judges 14:1-4 ESV)

As Judges 14 continues, we learn that God had a plan to use Samson's mistake as an opportunity for Samson to confront Israel's enemies, the Philistines. However, the marriage did not end well: Samson's wife betrayed him; he killed thirty Philistines; and she ended up with another man (Judges 14:15-20). If you try to do what is right in your eyes, not God's, the matter never ends well for anyone involved.

Benefits of a God-Fearing Wife

A God-fearing wife, by contrast, makes for a contented, functional home and healthy family life. Scripture highlights the substantial benefits of fearing God.

It is the foundation of wisdom. (Proverbs 1:7)

God grants wisdom to those who fear and honor him as God. The wisdom of God is essential to sound, effective family decision-making.

It motivates people to holiness, avoiding evil. (Proverbs 3:7)

THE ULTIMATE WIFE

The fear of God will help both you and your spouse to steer clear of sin and live a holy life, which brings blessings upon your family. Fear of God keeps you from unfaithfulness and deception, helping you to live honest, transparent lives.

It produces a sense of security for you and your family.
(Proverbs 14:26)

The fear of God brings confidence in God's divine protection. The righteous believer Job, from the Old Testament, enjoyed material wealth and other blessings, which further fueled his faith:

> Then the LORD said to Satan, "Have you considered my servant Job? There is no one on earth like him; he is blameless and upright, a man who fears God and shuns evil." **9** "Does Job fear God for nothing?" Satan replied. **10** "Have you not put a hedge around him and his household and everything he has? You have blessed the work of his hands, so that his flocks and herds are spread throughout the land."
> (Job 1:8-10 NIV)

When evil afterward beset Job's life, his confident faith carried him through, and God preserved him. In

THE ULTIMATE WIFE

due time, God bestowed every manner of blessing on Job and his family in even greater abundance than before (Job 42:12).

It makes all of life better. (Proverbs 15:16)

The fear of God improves the quality of your life and your marital relationship, no matter how much or how little you may possess materially at the moment.

It prolongs life. (Proverbs 10:27)

The fear of God is the ultimate life insurance policy, for God is the source of life in every sense.

It brings great blessings. (Proverbs 22:4)

Humility before God brings material wealth, a virtuous character, and spiritual health as well as physical safety. If you wish to build a strong, happy, healthy family, you must make God the bedrock of your marriage. Then, no matter what challenges you and your wife may face together, remember what David said:

> You, LORD, are my shepherd.
> I will never be in need.
> **2** You let me rest in fields
> of green grass.
> You lead me to streams

THE ULTIMATE WIFE

of peaceful water,
3 and you refresh my life.
You are true to your name,
and you lead me
along the right paths.
4 I may walk through valleys
as dark as death,
but I won't be afraid.
You are with me,
and your shepherd's rod
makes me feel safe.
5 You treat me to a feast,
while my enemies watch.
You honor me as your guest,
and you fill me cup
until it overflows.
6 Your kindness and love
will always be with me
each day of my life,
and I will live forever
in your house, Lord.
(Psalm 23:1-6 CEV)

CHAPTER TWO

She Loves Unconditionally

Love is an abstract noun. Though you cannot see love directly, you can feel it. When you are choosing your wife, therefore, after determining whether she is God-fearing, you should next consider true love.

In Proverbs 31:11-12, the queen describes the love of a good wife:

> Her husband has full confidence in her
> and lacks nothing of value.
> **12** She brings him good, not harm,
> all the days of her life. (NIV)

In order to have "full confidence" in someone, you must necessarily be assured of that person's complete

THE ULTIMATE WIFE

and unconditional love. Love plays a vital role in every successful relationship. You should marry a wife who truly loves you for who you are and what you are—not for who she imagines you are or wants you to become. If a woman naturally loves you from her heart, you will have a strong family because nothing will separate you and your spouse.

True love means that you want to remain by the other person's side no matter the circumstances. Such love imitates the love of Christ, which no amount of strain or hardship can weaken, as Paul explains in Romans 8:35-39:

> Who shall separate us from the love of Christ? Shall tribulation, or distress, or persecution, or famine, or nakedness, or peril, or sword?
> **36** As it is written, For thy sake we are killed all the day long; we are accounted as sheep for the slaughter.
> **37** Nay, in all these things we are more than conquerors through him that loved us.
> **38** For I am persuaded, that neither death, nor life, nor angels, nor principalities, nor powers, nor things present, nor things to come,
> **39** Nor height, nor depth, nor any other creature, shall be able to separate us from the

THE ULTIMATE WIFE

love of God, which is in Christ Jesus our Lord. (KJV)

This is how love is supposed to be—enduring in all seasons and situations. The word "love" is one of the most abused words in the English language, cheapened by careless use; and in any language, "love" is easy to say but difficult to practice. Since we invoke the word so casually, only time can tell if somebody truly loves you or not.

Sometimes you might be tempted to put pressure on a woman to say that she loves you, or vice versa. Being told that a woman loves you offers a sense of worth and security. The proof, however, is in her actions and speech over time. Coercing a woman into telling you that she loves you is unwise and risky. Let her express her love from her heart, if any when she chooses, but don't demand any such gesture; for if you do, you cannot be certain of her sincerity.

Instead, invest time in her, growing to know her heart better and allowing her to know you likewise. According to Paul, these behaviors are the chief signifiers of true love:

> Love is patient and kind. Love is not jealous or boastful or proud **5** or rude. It does not demand

THE ULTIMATE WIFE

its own way. It is not irritable, and it keeps no record of being wronged. **6** It does not rejoice about injustice but rejoices whenever the truth wins out. **7** Love never gives up, never loses faith, is always hopeful, and endures through every circumstance.
(1 Corinthians 13:4-7 NLT)

Delilah's Betrayal of Samson

You certainly don't need a woman like Delilah, who manipulated Samson and sold him out to his enemies, the Philistines. If you do not wait patiently for a woman who loves you genuinely from her heart, then you are only setting yourself up for betrayal. Some women will only love you for fleeting reasons, such as your appearance or your material possessions or some particular aspect of your personality. When these superficial elements disappear, or when this woman has satisfied her passing needs, then your relationship will end. Samson learned this lesson the hard way:

> After this he loved a woman in the Valley of Sorek, whose name was Delilah. **5** And the lords of the Philistines came up to her and said to her, "Seduce him, and see where his great strength lies, and by what means we may

THE ULTIMATE WIFE

overpower him, that we may bind him to humble him. And we will each give you 1,100 pieces of silver." **6** So Delilah said to Samson, "Please tell me where your great strength lies, and how you might be bound, that one could subdue you."

7 Samson said to her, "If they bind me with seven fresh bowstrings that have not been dried, then I shall become weak and be like any other man." **8** Then the lords of the Philistines brought up to her seven fresh bowstrings that had not been dried, and she bound him with them. **9** Now she had men lying in ambush in an inner chamber. And she said to him, "The Philistines are upon you, Samson!" But he snapped the bowstrings, as a thread of flax snaps when it touches the fire. So the secret of his strength was not known.

10 Then Delilah said to Samson, "Behold, you have mocked me and told me lies. Please tell me how you might be bound." **11** And he said to her, "If they bind me with new ropes that have not been used, then I shall become weak and be like any other man." **12** So Delilah took new ropes and bound him with them and said to him, "The Philistines are upon you, Samson!"

THE ULTIMATE WIFE

And the men lying in ambush were in an inner chamber. But he snapped the ropes off his arms like a thread.
13 Then Delilah said to Samson, "Until now you have mocked me and told me lies. Tell me how you might be bound." And he said to her, "If you weave the seven locks of my head with the web and fasten it tight with the pin, then I shall become weak and be like any other man." **14** So while he slept, Delilah took the seven locks of his head and wove them into the web. And she made them tight with the pin and said to him, "The Philistines are upon you, Samson!" But he awoke from his sleep and pulled away the pin, the loom, and the web.
15 And she said to him, "How can you say, 'I love you,' when your heart is not with me? You have mocked me these three times, and you have not told me where your great strength lies." **16** And when she pressed him hard with her words day after day, and urged him, his soul was vexed to death. **17** And he told her all his heart, and said to her, "A razor has never come upon my head, for I have been a Nazirite to God from my mother's womb. If my head is shaved, then my strength will leave me, and I

THE ULTIMATE WIFE

shall become weak and be like any other man." **18** When Delilah saw that he had told her all his heart, she sent and called the lords of the Philistines, saying, "Come up again, for he has told me all his heart." Then the lords of the Philistines came up to her and brought the money in their hands. **19** She made him sleep on her knees. And she called a man and had him shave off the seven locks of his head. Then she began to torment him, and his strength left him. **20** And she said, "The Philistines are upon you, Samson!" And he awoke from his sleep and said, "I will go out as at other times and shake myself free." But he did not know that the LORD had left him.

Biblical True-Love

The word "love" is a short word, yet it is immensely powerful when someone speaks it sincerely from his or her heart. If a woman habitually threatens to leave you should you fail to meet some condition or ultimatum, then she does not love you as a wife should love a husband. True love is not conditional. Likewise, if a woman continually asks things of you, as Delilah did of Samson, then be careful. Though true love takes time to find and longer to verify, the right woman will remain

THE ULTIMATE WIFE

with you forever once you find her.

Biblical true-love places others above oneself:

> Therefore, if there is any encouragement in Christ, any comfort in love, any sharing in the Spirit, any sympathy, **2** complete my joy by thinking the same way, being united, and agreeing with each other. **3** Don't do anything for selfish purposes, but with humility think of others as better than yourselves. **4** Instead of each person watching out for their own good, watch out for what is better for others. 5 Adopt the attitude that was in Christ Jesus...
> (Philippians 2:1-5 CEB)

This is the sort of selfless or other-oriented love that you must have for your wife, and she for you. The Bible describes true love as driving away fear and bringing peace in its stead:

> ...God is love. If we keep on loving others, we will stay one in our hearts with God, and he will stay one with us. **17** If we truly love others and live as Christ did in this world, we won't be worried about the day of judgment. **18** A real love for others will chase those worries away.

THE ULTIMATE WIFE

> The thought of being punished is what makes us afraid. It shows that we have not really learned to love.
> (1 John 4:16-18 CEV)

If you are afraid that the woman with whom you are in a relationship will leave you and, because of that, you accept everything she does, then you are not in a relationship defined by true love. Spouses should be able to correct each other, or suggest areas in which the other person needs to improve, without getting into trouble—though, of course, this must be done lovingly and respectfully.

Is it difficult to find someone who will truly love you? Keep in mind that such love doesn't develop overnight but in the course of a gradual process. Therefore, although true love is not just a theory or a figment of a writer's imagination, neither is it the trite, fictionalized fare of romantic comedies. True love can occur in day-to-day reality, too; but you must start with friendship and work to develop a fully-fledged, romantic true-love relationship that will last.

This must be accomplished patiently and with honesty, not fearfully pretending to be someone you are not. True love is built upon trust and commitment. True love is when you discover your best friend and can

THE ULTIMATE WIFE

be yourself around her. It's when words cannot fully express your feelings toward her but you know beyond a doubt that God intended you for her and she for you. You would wait forever to be with her.

In the realm of romantic relationships, to love someone is nothing; to be loved by someone is something; to love someone who loves you is everything. Love isn't all about flirting, hugs, kisses, and sex. Love, rather, is when you can remove all of those things from the equation yet never waver in your feelings, commitment, or devotion to one another.

CHAPTER THREE

She Uses Godly Speech

In Proverbs 31, the queen tells her son to consider a wife who chooses her words carefully. Bathsheba describes the speaking habits of the virtuous wife thus: "Her words are sensible, and her advice is thoughtful" (Proverbs 31:26 CEV). Why is it important for you to find a wife who speaks sensibly? Remember that you are looking for a lifelong friend and companion—someone who completes you as your other half and who provides you with comfort and counsel.

For Better and for Worse

You are looking for someone who will be there for you even during trying times, so the words that a woman speaks in difficult moments will affect your relationship, your family, and your home. An

THE ULTIMATE WIFE

anonymously written poem explains the importance of wise speech in this way:

> A careless word may kindle strife;
> A cruel word may wreck a life.
> A timely word may level stress,
> But a loving word may heal and bless.

I doubt that you would wish for a woman like Job's wife, who told her husband to curse God and die. When her husband was rich and in good health, she certainly did not ask her husband to curse God; but when trouble arrived, she was quick to blame Him:

> His wife said to him, "Are you still maintaining your integrity? Curse God and die!"
> **10** He replied, "You are talking like a foolish woman. Shall we accept good from God, and not trouble?"
> (Job 2:9-10 NIV)

Some women only want to share the pleasant seasons of smooth sailing with you. If a woman is willing to curse God, who created her, then how much quicker do you think she will be to resent you, a mere man? When a person is angry, the tongue is difficult to control.

THE ULTIMATE WIFE

However, if you are a believer, your speech will maintain certain limits instinctively even in your worst moments. A believer is mindful of his or her words.

Job was truly in deep trouble at the time, and no doubt he wished for someone to comfort him; yet all that his own wife could do was advise him to speak against God. The following passage describes what Job was going through:

> One day when Job's sons and daughters were feasting and drinking wine at the oldest brother's house, **14** a messenger came to Job and said, "The oxen were plowing and the donkeys were grazing nearby, **15** and the Sabeans attacked and made off with them. They put the servants to the sword, and I am the only one who has escaped to tell you!"
> **16** While he was still speaking, another messenger came and said, "The fire of God fell from the heavens and burned up the sheep and the servants, and I am the only one who has escaped to tell you!"
> **17** While he was still speaking, another messenger came and said, "The Chaldeans formed three raiding parties and swept down on your camels and made off with them. They put

THE ULTIMATE WIFE

the servants to the sword, and I am the only one who has escaped to tell you!"
18 While he was still speaking, yet another messenger came and said, "Your sons and daughters were feasting and drinking wine at the oldest brother's house, **19** when suddenly a mighty wind swept in from the desert and struck the four corners of the house. It collapsed on them and they are dead, and I am the only one who has escaped to tell you!"
20 At this, Job got up and tore his robe and shaved his head. Then he fell to the ground in worship **21** and said:
"Naked I came from my mother's womb,
and naked I will depart.
The Lord gave and the Lord has taken away;
may the name of the Lord be praised."
(Job 1:13-22 NIV)

As Job probably realized, a person's words are an excellent gauge of his or her general character. Jesus affirmed this truth:

> "Make a tree good and its fruit will be good, or make a tree bad and its fruit will be bad, for a tree is recognized by its fruit. **34** You brood of

THE ULTIMATE WIFE

vipers, how can you who are evil say anything good? *For the mouth speaks what the heart is full of.*" (Matthew 12:33-34 NIV)

Speech That Kills versus Speech That Heals

If a woman cannot control herself when she is angry, be wary. Christians and non-Christians alike seem to use the same words these days, which is troubling. Language is powerful and not to be used lightly. Words can destroy you or bring you success, life, and all kinds of blessing. Proverbs 18:21 declares, "Death and life are in the power of the tongue, and those who love it will eat its fruits" (ESV). You must therefore pray that the Lord will guide you to a wife who is respectful and thoughtful.

The book of James describes the tongue as full of deadly poison and, thus, as something dangerous that we must tame. When we are angry, the words that can issue from our mouths are sufficient to kill or destroy as surely as poison. James explained the destruction that a person's words can bring not only upon others but also upon himself or herself:

> We all make mistakes often, but those who don't make mistakes with their words have reached full maturity. Like a bridled horse, they

THE ULTIMATE WIFE

can control themselves entirely. **3** When we bridle horses and put in their mouths to lead them wherever we want, we can control their whole bodies.

4 Consider ships: They are so large that strong winds are needed to drive them. But pilots direct their ships wherever they want with a little rudder. **5** In the same way, even though the tongue is a small part of the body, it boasts wildly.

Think about this: A small flame can set a whole forest on fire. **6** The tongue is a small flame of fire, a world of evil at work in us. It contaminates our entire lives. Because of it, the circle of life is set on fire. The tongue itself is set on fire by the flames of hell.

7 People can tame and already have tamed every kind of animal, bird, reptile, and fish. **8** No one can tame the tongue, though. It is a restless evil, full of deadly poison. **9** With it we both bless the Lord and Father and curse human beings made in God's likeness. **10** Blessing and cursing come from the same mouth. My brothers and sisters, it just shouldn't be this way!

11 Both fresh water and salt water don't come from the same spring, do they?

THE ULTIMATE WIFE

(James 3:2-11 CEB)

If a woman tosses words about carelessly, then you will struggle to live a peaceful and happy life together. Unfortunately, most people don't take words seriously and, because of that, their own words will destroy them. Words lead people into trouble, which is why the Bible says that we should not even joke with certain words. Jesus explained the consequences:

> "A good man brings good things out of the good stored up in him, and an evil man brings evil things out of the evil stored up in him. **36** But I tell you that everyone will have to give account on the Day of Judgment for every empty word they have spoken. **37** For by your words you will be acquitted, and by your words you will be condemned."

(Matthew 12:35-37 NIV)

You need a wife who can encourage, motivate, and advise you as needed. This is in accordance with Ephesians 4:29, which instructs, "Let no corrupting talk come out of your mouths, but only such as is good for building up, as fits the occasion, that it may give grace to those who hear" (ESV).

THE ULTIMATE WIFE

Wise words bring healing. As Proverbs 12:18 explains, "There is one whose rash words are like sword thrusts, but the tongue of the wise brings healing." Proverbs 16:24 elaborates, saying, "Gracious words are like a honeycomb, sweetness to the soul and health to the body." By contrast, according to Colossians 3:8, "you must put them all away: anger, wrath, malice, slander, and obscene talk from your mouth." (ESV)

Ill-considered words, meanwhile, destroy life. Proverbs 15:2 states, plainly yet truly, "Words of wisdom come from the wise, but fools speak foolishness" (CEV). In particular, corrupt and ungodly language kills. As Proverbs 15:4 observes, "A gentle tongue is a tree of life, but perverseness in it breaks the spirit" (ESV).

Unholy speech features prominently throughout this list of seven things that God—who is the God of love—deeply hates:

> These six things the Lord hates,
> Yes, seven are an abomination to Him:
> **17** A proud look,
> A lying tongue,
> Hands that shed innocent blood,
> **18** A heart that devises wicked plans,
> Feet that are swift in running to evil,

THE ULTIMATE WIFE

19 A false witness who speaks lies,
And one who sows discord among brethren.
(Proverbs 6:16-19 NKJV)

The Immoral Woman versus the Virtuous Wife

Proverbs 5 offers fatherly advice about women to a young man. A prominent theme in this chapter, and throughout the book of Proverbs, is the contrast between a wicked woman—"the immoral woman"—and a proper, loving wife. Note that both types of women are beautiful, but the beauty of the wicked woman is deceptive while the latter's is enduring:

> My son, pay attention to my wisdom;
> Lend your ear to my understanding,
> **2** That you may preserve discretion,
> And your lips may keep knowledge.
> **3** For the lips of an immoral woman drip honey,
> and her mouth [speech] *is* smoother than oil;
> **4** But in the end she is bitter as wormwood,
> Sharp as a two-edged sword.
> **5** Her feet go down to death,
> Her steps lay hold of hell.
> **6** Lest you ponder *her* path of life—
> Her ways are unstable;
> You do not know *them*.

THE ULTIMATE WIFE

7 Therefore hear me now, *my* children,
And do not depart from the words of my mouth.
8 Remove your way far from her,
And do not go near the door of her house,
9 Lest you give your honor to others,
And your years to the cruel *one*;
10 Lest aliens [strangers] be filled with your wealth,
And your labors *go* to the house of a foreigner;
11 And you mourn at last,
When your flesh and your body are consumed,
12 And say:
"How I have hated instruction,
And my heart despised correction!
. . . **15** Drink water from your own cistern,
And running water from your own well.
16 Should your fountains be dispersed abroad,
Streams of water in the streets?
17 Let them be only your own,
And not for strangers with you.
18 Let your fountain be blessed,
And rejoice with the wife of your youth.
19 *As a* loving deer and a graceful doe,
Let her breasts satisfy you at all times;
And always be enraptured with her love.

THE ULTIMATE WIFE

> **20** For why should you, my son, be enraptured by an immoral woman,
> And be embraced in the arms of a seductress?
> **21** For the ways of man *are* before the eyes of the LORD,
> And He ponders all his paths.
> **22** His own iniquities trap the wicked *man*,
> And he is caught in the cords of his sin.
> **23** He shall die for lack of instruction,
> And in the greatness of his folly he shall go astray.
> (Proverbs 5:1-12, 15-23 NKJV, emphasis in original)

Paul sums up the characteristics of a virtuous wife in Titus 2:4-5, advising believers to speak in such a way…

> …that they may train the young women to love their husbands, to love their children,
> **5** to be sober-minded, chaste, workers at home, kind, being in subjection to their own husbands, that the word of God be not blasphemed…
> (ASV)

Therefore, pay close attention to the words that your future wife speaks, both when she is cheerful and when

THE ULTIMATE WIFE

she is upset. A wife should use words to build up and motivate her husband, children, and others. If you are experiencing tough times, as Job did, then you want to a wife by your side who will encourage you and cheer you up. Some women are in the habit of cutting others down with their words, but they should learn from those women who excel at lifting up the spirits of men in the face of hardship.

CHAPTER FOUR

She is Industrious

The Bible commands us to work, which is why God put the first man He created, Adam, to work in the Garden of Eden. Many people have the false impression that Adam and Eve were allowed to kick back and relax in those early days, as if they were on permanent vacation in an earthly paradise. However, God created man to work with Him in the world (Genesis 2:8). God planted a garden and put Adam there to cultivate and maintain it—"to work it and keep it" (Genesis 2:15 ESV). Moreover, Adam and Eve were to "subdue" the earth and "have dominion" over its other creatures (Genesis 1:28 ESV). In other words, God created mankind to manage resources in a position of responsibility that required discipline.

Apostle Paul had this to say about work in his second

THE ULTIMATE WIFE

letter to the Thessalonians:

> For even when we were with you, we would give you this command: If anyone is not willing to work, let him not eat. **11** For we hear that some among you walk in idleness, not busy at work, but busybodies. **12** Now such persons we command and encourage in the Lord Jesus Christ to do their work quietly and to earn their own living.
> (2 Thessalonians 3:10-12 ESV)

As you pray for your future wife, and as you find her and gradually build your relationship, you must also be gainfully employed in some manner. That way, you will be able to provide materially for your future family. Avoid dependence upon a woman's money—not because women should not earn money but because it is not healthy for the head of a household to rely on his wife for food and shelter.

Furthermore, hard work is simply a good habit for believers. Paul wrote in Ephesians 4:28, "Let the thief no longer steal, but rather let him labor, doing honest work with his own hands, so that he may have something to share with anyone in need" (ESV).

THE ULTIMATE WIFE

Manager of the Household

The queen in Proverbs also addresses the matter of work. Bathsheba told her son to consider a wife who is a hard worker. This doesn't mean, however, that you ought to marry an office worker or businesswoman. In the olden days, most women were housewives—and I dare you to tell any dedicated housewife that she does not work. In many ways, maintaining a home and family is far more difficult than office work. A housewife deserves at least as much respect as a full-time worker. The queen identified several types of labor involved in managing a household:

> She finds wool and flax
> and busily spins it.
> **14** She is like a merchant's ship,
> bringing her food from afar.
> **15** She gets up before dawn to prepare breakfast for her household
> and plan the day's work for her servant girls.
> **16** She goes to inspect a field and buys it;
> with her earnings she plants a vineyard.
> **17** She is energetic and strong,
> a hard worker.
> **18** She makes sure her dealings are profitable;
> her lamp burns late into the night.

THE ULTIMATE WIFE

(Proverbs 31:13-18 NLT)

You can see from these verses that the queen wanted her son to marry an industrious woman who did not shy from hard work. Though such a woman is to be held in higher regard than that of unpaid domestic help, she maintains a servant's heart and is willing to work without complaint. An industrious wife labors from her heart and readily offers her best all the time. She constantly looks for solutions to problem rather than depending solely upon, or finding fault with, others.

The apostle Paul therefore emphasized in Titus 2:4 that young women should be trained to be virtuous "workers at home" (ASV). Similarly, in 1 Timothy 5:14, he advised, "So I counsel younger widows to marry, to have children, *to manage their homes* and to give the enemy no opportunity for slander" (NIV).

Provider for Her Family

The queen in Proverbs 31 says that a wife ought to wake up early and prepare food for her family (Proverbs 31:15). Modern women, however, often struggle in the kitchen. I have heard some women confidently and unabashedly state that they don't know how to cook. The truth, though, is that cooking does not number among the spiritual gifts mentioned in the Bible. This

THE ULTIMATE WIFE

means that cooking is a talent that anyone can learn. If a woman informs you that she doesn't know how to cook and is not willing to learn, then alarm bells should sound in your head. According to the queen's advice, an excellent wife should be able to cook for her own family.

Although, especially in a large household, a wife may require hired help, she should not delegate the responsibility of cooking for her own husband. Food is essential for the human body, so if your potential wife lacks the time or inclination to cook for her family and plans to leave all of the food preparation to you or to a servant, her priorities are likely amiss.

Some women consider cooking to be menial or dirty work. They may worry more about their nails or someplace they would rather be than in the kitchen. Other women are simply too lazy to plan and fix meals for their families. If a woman is not a "morning person," that is no excuse; she could prepare breakfast the night before. In Proverbs 6:6-11, the Bible has this to say about laziness:

> Take a lesson from the ants, you lazybones.
> Learn from their ways and become wise!
> 7 Though they have no prince
> or governor or ruler to make them work,

THE ULTIMATE WIFE

8 they labor hard all summer,
gathering food for the winter.
9 But you, lazybones, how long will you sleep? When will you wake up?
10 A little extra sleep, a little more slumber, a little folding of the hands to rest—
11 then poverty will pounce on you like a bandit; scarcity will attack you like an armed robber. (NLT)

Proverbs 10:4 adds that laziness leads to poverty while hard work brings wealth. On that note, do not hesitate to share in household chores. To do so is a beautiful and godly example to your children and a gesture of loving companionship to your wife. Moreover, do not deny your wife the opportunity to work outside the home, or to otherwise seek gainful employment, if she can best support your family in that way. Nowhere does the Bible state that women should not work, whether inside or outside of the home.

Nowadays, women are allowed to do most of the same jobs as men. Even in the olden days, however, women had certain opportunities for work apart from the business of housewivery. Although some men force their wives to stop working, this is not a biblical proscription. In fact, you and your wife could operate a

THE ULTIMATE WIFE

business together as did Priscilla and her husband Aquila, according to Acts 18. If you have children and you think that your wife ought to remain home for the sake of your kids, then be prepared to respect fully her work in the home.

Next we will introduce some of the biblical women who worked hard in capacities other than, or in addition to, being housewives.

Service outside the Home

Rachel, the wife of Isaac, was a shepherd before she married her husband. Genesis 29:9 relates, "While he was still talking with them, Rachel came with her father's sheep, for she was a shepherd" (NIV).

Rhoda was a domestic servant at the house where Peter went after his miraculous escape from Herod Agrippa's prison (Acts 12:13).

Priscilla and her husband, Aquila, were members of the early church who also labored together as "tentmakers" (Acts 18:3 NIV):

> After this, Paul left Athens and went to Corinth. 2 There he found a Jew named Aquila, a native of Pontus. He had recently come from Italy with his wife Priscilla because Claudius had ordered all Jews to leave Rome. Paul visited

THE ULTIMATE WIFE

with them, **3** Because they practiced the same trade, he stayed and worked with them. They all worked with leather.
(Acts 18:1-3 CEB)

Some women were also professional mourners, specially trained to express grief through song on behalf of the community. Jeremiah 9:17 refers to such women: "This is what the Lord Almighty says: 'Consider now! Call for the wailing women to come; send for the most skillful of them'" (NIV).

Caring for Children
Shiphrah and Puah were midwives during the period of the Hebrews' enslavement in Egypt, and they were God-fearing women:

> Then Pharaoh, the king of Egypt, gave this order to the Hebrew midwives, Shiphrah and Puah: **16** "When you help the Hebrew women as they give birth, watch as they deliver. If the baby is a boy, kill him; if it is a girl, let her live." **17** But because the midwives feared God, they refused to obey the king's orders. They allowed the boys to live, too.
> (Exodus 1:15-17 NLT)

THE ULTIMATE WIFE

Throughout the Old Testament, the Bible speaks of nurses— women who cared for children, particularly those from wealthier families, and who often remained their servants as the children grew up. The following passages offer examples of such nurses:

> Now Deborah, Rebekah's nurse, died and was buried under the oak outside Bethel. So it was named Allon Bakuth.
> (Genesis 35:8 NIV)

> Then his [Moses'] sister said to Pharaoh's daughter, "Shall I go and call you a nurse from the Hebrew women to nurse the child for you?"
> (Exodus 2:7 ESV)

> Jonathan, the son of Saul, had a son who was crippled in his feet. He was five years old when the news about Saul and Jonathan came from Jezreel, and his nurse took him up and fled, and as she fled in her haste, he fell and became lame. And his name was Mephibosheth.
> (2 Samuel 4:4 ESV)

Leadership in Ministry and Business

THE ULTIMATE WIFE

Joanna, the wife of King Herod's household steward, was among the women who supported Jesus' ministry financially:

> After this, Jesus traveled about from one town and village to another, proclaiming the good news of the kingdom of God. The Twelve were with him, **2** and also some women who had been cured of evil spirits and diseases: Mary (called Magdalene) from whom seven demons had come out; **3** *Joanna the wife of Chuza, the manager of Herod's household*; Susanna; and many others. These women were helping to support them out of their own means.
> (Luke 8:1-3 NIV)

Lydia was a successful businesswoman and a devoted woman of God. Acts 16:14 recounts, "One of those listening was a woman from the city of Thyatira named Lydia, a dealer in purple cloth. She was a worshiper of God. The Lord opened her heart to respond to Paul's message" (NIV).

Spiritual Leadership

Deborah was a prophetess, wife, and judge—that is, she was one of the great military leaders of the Israelites

THE ULTIMATE WIFE

prior to the founding of the monarchy:

> Now Deborah, a prophet, the wife of Lappidoth, was leading Israel at that time. **5** She held court under the Palm of Deborah between Ramah and Bethel in the hill country of Ephraim, and the Israelites went up to her to have their disputes decided. **6** She sent for Barak son of Abinoam from Kedesh in Naphtali and said to him, "The LORD, the God of Israel, commands you: 'Go, take with you ten thousand men of Naphtali and Zebulun and lead them up to Mount Tabor. **7** I will lead Sisera, the commander of Jabin's army, with his chariots and his troops to the Kishon River and give him into your hands.'"

8 Barak said to her, "If you go with me, I will go; but if you don't go with me, I won't go."

9 "Certainly I will go with you," said Deborah. "But because of the course you are taking, the honor will not be yours, for the LORD will deliver Sisera into the hands of a woman." So Deborah went with Barak to Kedesh. **10** There Barak summoned Zebulun and Naphtali, and ten thousand men went up under his command. Deborah also went up with him.

THE ULTIMATE WIFE

(Judges 4:4-10 NIV)

Other prophetesses appear in the Old Testament as well. Powerful men consulted these women for spiritual advice, as when King Josiah sought counsel on what to do with the recently rediscovered book of Mosaic law:

> So Hilkiah the priest, and Ahikam, and Achbor, and Shaphan, and Asahiah went to Huldah the *prophetess*, the wife of Shallum the son of Tikvah, son of Harhas, keeper of the wardrobe; (now she lived in Jerusalem in the Second Quarter), and they talked with her.
> (2 Kings 22:14 ESV)

In the New Testament, we learn that Priscilla and her husband, Aquila, the tentmakers, were devoted friends and ministry colleagues of Paul:

> Meanwhile, a certain Jew named Apollos arrived in Ephesus. He was a native of Alexandria and was well-educated and effective in his use of the scriptures. **25** He had been instructed in the way of the Lord and spoke as one stirred up by the Spirit. He taught accurately the things about Jesus, even though he was aware only of the

THE ULTIMATE WIFE

baptism John proclaimed and practiced. **26** He began speaking with confidence in the synagogue. *When Priscilla and Aquila heard him, they received him into their circle of friends and explained to him God's way more accurately.*
(Acts 18:24-26 CEB)

Their home served as a meeting place for believers. At some point, they even risked their lives for Paul's sake:

Say hello to Priscilla and Aquila, my coworkers in Christ Jesus, **4** who risked their own necks for my life. I'm not the only one who thanks God for them, but all the churches of the Gentiles do the same. **5** Also say hello to the church that meets in their house...
(Romans 16:3-5 CEB)

Phoebe was another woman who earned Paul's respect as a leader in the early church:

I have good things to say about Phoebe, who is a leader in the church at Cenchreae. **2** Welcome her in a way that is proper for someone who has faith in the Lord and is one of God's own

THE ULTIMATE WIFE

people. Help her in any way you can. After all, she has proved to be a respected leader for many others, including me.
(Romans 16:1-2 CEV)

These women worked hard to support their families. You ought to pray for such a wife—for a woman who will serve as your helper and partner in providing for each other and the rest of your family. An industrious wife brings happiness and contentment to your life.

CHAPTER FIVE

She Dresses Modestly

Are matters of clothing truly important in choosing your future wife? While this is not as critical an issue as the others we have examined so far, attire is nonetheless indicative of character to some extent and, therefore, is worthy of consideration.

The clothing worn in biblical times differs from what we wear today. Both men and women wore a loose, woolen, robe-like cloak or mantle as an outer garment. It was fastened at the waist with a belt or sash. A tunic or coat made of cloth, leather, or haircloth was worn under the cloak. Men and women alike wore sandals on their feet.

Wearing Too Little—The Dangers of Indecency

In modern times, clothing oneself has become more

THE ULTIMATE WIFE

complicated and more of a challenge. In the olden days, you would be able to identify people's country, culture, and religious affiliation by their attire. Due to increased freedom, mass-market culture, and globalization, most people can choose to wear nearly anything they want, nearly anytime they like.

The world around us promotes full freedom of expression in clothing, and Christians largely follow the ways of the world in this regard. Distinct Christian notions of beauty and propriety in appearance have become difficult to identify. In the book of Romans, however, the apostle Paul offers a Christian perspective on these matters:

> Dear friends, God is good. So I beg you to offer your bodies to him as a living sacrifice, pure and pleasing. That's the most sensible way to serve God. 2 *Don't be like the people of this world, but let God change the way you think.* Then you will know how to do everything that is good and pleasing to him.
> (Romans 12:1-2 CEV)

Jesus, too, clarified that even though we as believers live in this world for now, we not ultimately of this world:

THE ULTIMATE WIFE

I have told them your message. But the people of this world hate them, because they don't belong to this world, just as I don't.
15 Father, I don't ask you to take my followers out of the world, but keep them safe from the evil one. **16** They don't belong to this world, and neither do I.
(John 17:14-16 CEV)

In our present era and society, dressing oneself trends toward exposing as much as possible, including parts of the body that ought not be seen by anyone other than a spouse. People cloth their bodies—or don't, as the case may be—so as to glorify themselves, not God.

In describing the mode of dress appropriate for women in church, Paul exhorts them to dress "modestly" with "decency and propriety" (1 Timothy 2:9 NIV). He then proceeds to contrast immodest dress with the good deeds that are appropriate for women who profess to be true worshipers of God:

> In the same way, I want women to enhance their appearance with clothing that is modest and sensible, not with elaborate hairstyles, gold, pearls, or expensive clothes. **10** They should

THE ULTIMATE WIFE

make themselves attractive by doing good, which is appropriate for women who claim to honor God.

(1 Timothy 2:9-10 CEB)

Modesty in the way we dress is not only for church; it is to be the standard for all Christians at all times. The key to understanding what constitutes modesty in dress is to examine the attitudes and intents of the heart. Those whose hearts are inclined toward God will make every effort to dress modestly, decently, and appropriately to the occasion.

The queen in Proverbs, describing a "truly good wife," says, "She does her own sewing, and everything she wears is beautiful" (Proverbs 31:10, 22 CEV). In other words, no one tells a virtuous woman what to wear. Ideally, she is not even bound to the clothing options created by others but, rather, fashions her own attire. Her clothing choices are based on what is prudent and right, but they are nonetheless beautiful.

The Body as the Temple of God

The Bible refers to the human body as the temple of God. Paul asked the Corinthians, "Or don't you know that your body is a temple of the Holy Spirit who is in you? Don't you know that you have the Holy Spirit

THE ULTIMATE WIFE

from God, and you don't belong to yourselves?" (1 Corinthians 6:19 CEB). Therefore, a Christian lady must cover her body so as to show respect for our Lord Jesus Christ.

> God created the body—your body, and that of every believer—for Himself. The physical body is His creation, and every believer's body represents the church, of which He is the head. Paul emphasized this in saying, "Food is for the stomach and the stomach for food, and yet God will do away with both. The body isn't for sexual immorality but for the Lord, and the Lord for the body" (1 Corinthians 6:13 CEB).

The body of every man and woman is to be treated literally as a part of Christ: "Don't you know that your bodies are part of the body of Christ? Is it right for me to join part of the body of Christ to a prostitute? No, it isn't! (1 Corinthians 6:15 CEV). Instead of displaying her body in a way that gratifies impure human desires, then, a woman ought always to present herself in a way that glorifies God. As Paul explained, "God paid a great price for you. So use your body to honor God" (1 Corinthians 6:20 CEV).

Bible recognizes that prostitutes and other women of

THE ULTIMATE WIFE

unwholesome purpose have a particular way of dressing. For instance, Proverbs 7:10 says, "Then out came a woman to meet him, dressed like a prostitute and with crafty intent" (NIV). Prostitutes dress to attract men, which is why they expose their bodies. If you meet a woman who is not a prostitute yet dresses like one, then you ought to take pause before considering her as a potential spouse.

The Scriptures prescribe modest dress for women in particular, but what exactly does that mean in the context of modern society? Does it mean that a woman must be covered from head to toe? Certain cults and other religions require women to cover their entire bodies. While the apostle Paul told Christian women to cover their heads in church, historical and cultural context do play a legitimate role, to some extent, in determining standards of attire. In the ancient Near and Middle East, covering the head was an expression of modesty. If women do not cover their heads indoors in your culture, then doing so in church is not necessary.

Wearing Too Much—The Danger of Extravagance

A woman can dress fashionably without dressing extravagantly. Obsession with extravagant clothes and the latest fashions has turned some women into shopaholics. Such women are addicted to shopping and

THE ULTIMATE WIFE

derive enjoyment from buying clothes simply for the sake of buying them. While purchasing necessary things is proper, shopping in an uncontrolled, impulsive manner is not.

Shopaholics—including some men, not only women—are slaves to the consumerism and to the ephemeral whims of the fashion world. Debt often ensues, which leads to conflict in the home, especially if a shopaholic wife depends on her spouse to fund her addiction.

This is what the Bible says about extravagant clothing:

> Moreover, the LORD said, "Because the daughters of Zion are proud
> And walk with heads held high and seductive eyes,
> And go along with mincing steps
> And tinkle the bangles on their feet,
> **17** Therefore the Lord will afflict the scalp of the daughters of Zion with scabs,
> And the LORD will make their foreheads bare."
> **18** In that day the Lord will take away the beauty of their anklets, headbands, crescent ornaments,
> **19** dangling earrings, bracelets, veils,
> **20** headdresses, ankle chains, sashes, perfume

THE ULTIMATE WIFE

boxes, amulets, **21** finger rings, nose rings, **22** festal robes, outer tunics, cloaks, money purses, **23** hand mirrors, undergarments, turbans and veils.
24 Now it will come about that instead of sweet perfume there will be putrefaction;
Instead of a belt, a rope;
Instead of well-set hair, a plucked-out scalp;
Instead of fine clothes, a donning of sackcloth;
And branding instead of beauty.
25 Your men will fall by the sword
And your mighty ones in battle.
26 And her gates will lament and mourn,
And deserted she will sit on the ground.
(Isaiah 3:16-26 NASB)

In the New Testament, the apostle Peter makes clear that lasting beauty is a matter of inner gentleness and virtue, not "fancy hairdos" and "expensive clothes" (1 Peter 3:3-4 CEV).

Abigail, a Wife of Inner Beauty

Thus, from a biblical perspective, true beauty comes from within, not from the clothes and accessories with which a woman adorns herself. In searching for the ultimate wife, then, you should consider the inner

THE ULTIMATE WIFE

beauty of a woman more than her outward appearance. True beauty is a matter of character.

In the book of 1 Samuel, a woman named Abigail is described as "intelligent and beautiful," contrasting sharply with her husband:

> A certain man in Maon, who had property there at Carmel, was very wealthy. He had a thousand goats and three thousand sheep, which he was shearing in Carmel. **3** His name was Nabal and his wife's name was Abigail. *She was an intelligent and beautiful woman*, but her husband was surly and mean in his dealings—he was a Calebite.
> (1 Samuel 25:2-3 NIV)

Abigail is presented in the Bible as a woman worthy of respect—not because she was beautiful but because of the prudent action that she took on behalf of her husband. The incident is recorded in 1 Samuel 25:14-19:

> One of the servants told Abigail, Nabal's wife, "David sent messengers from the wilderness to give our master his greetings, but he hurled insults at them. **15** Yet these men were very good to us. They did not mistreat us, and the whole time we were out in the fields near them

THE ULTIMATE WIFE

nothing was missing. **16** Night and day they were a wall around us the whole time we were herding our sheep near them. **17** Now think it over and see what you can do, because disaster is hanging over our master and his whole household. He is such a wicked man that no one can talk to him."
18 Abigail acted quickly. She took two hundred loaves of bread, two skins of wine, five dressed sheep, five seahs of roasted grain, a hundred cakes of raisins and two hundred cakes of pressed figs, and loaded them on donkeys. **19** Then she told her servants, "Go on ahead; I'll follow you." But she did not tell her husband Nabal. (NIV)

In 1 Samuel 25:32-34, David makes clear that Abigail's intelligence or wisdom is her defining virtue, by which she saved her family and household:

David said to Abigail, "Praise be to the LORD, the God of Israel, who has sent you today to meet me. **33** May you be blessed for your good judgment and for keeping me from bloodshed this day and from avenging myself with my own hands. **34** Otherwise, as surely as the LORD, the

THE ULTIMATE WIFE

God of Israel, lives, who has kept me from harming you, if you had not come quickly to meet me, not one male belonging to Nabal would have been left alive by daybreak." (NIV)

Abigail is representative of a long tradition of female peacemakers. In Matthew 5:9, Jesus says, "Blessed are the peacemakers, for they will be called children of God" (NIV). When Abigail learned of her husband's folly, she responded with a peaceful approach. Rather than confront or chastize her husband for being rude to David and his servants, she took action to deescalate the situation. Abigail understood not only that the peaceful way is the better way but also that "peaceful" does not translate into "passive."

In searching for a wife, you need a woman with brains as well as beauty, like Abigail. Above all, a wife ought to possess confidently the beauty that comes from within. Such virtue is far more attractive and valuable than the insecure, superficial type of beauty that relies upon indecent or extravagant dress to convince others of a woman's worth.

CHAPTER SIX

She Loves Children

Most men want to have children when they get married. Always remember, though, that the main reason God instituted marriage was to provide a man with his best friend, lifelong companion, and complement. While children are important, they are not essential to marriage, nor should they be the main reason for two people to marry.

Unfortunately, beliefs to the contrary prompt some men to pressure their wives unduly to have baby. Some men use this as an excuse to divorce and pursue another women. Even Abraham and Sarah, the ancestors of the Israelites, became impatient for God's promise of a child and agreed that Abraham should try to produce a child through relations with Sarah's servant Hagar (Genesis 16:2). On the other hand, some women are honest from the beginning that, for some personal

THE ULTIMATE WIFE

reasons, they don't want to have babies. Others cannot bear children for physical reasons.

If you, as a man, deeply desire to have children but a woman informs you that she doesn't want kids, then she is not meant to be your wife. Perhaps you already have children and are looking for someone who would be a good mother to them. A woman could be perfect match in every other respect, but if she doesn't like kids, then keep looking.

Children are gift from God. The Bible says in Psalm 127:3, "Children are a gift from the LORD; they are a reward from him" (NLT). Therefore, if both you and your wife want children and are believers in Christ, you will wait upon the Lord. If you cannot have children on your own, then you can adopt children who are in need of a loving, faith-filled home.

Pray for a wife who loves children and will have time to help you raise a family. Especially since children tend to spend more time with their mothers, your future wife must love kids and be determined to provide a well-managed household for them.

Mothers profoundly influence their sons and daughters! One of life's greatest blessings is to have a godly mother. Sadly, the influence of the feminist movement has diminished the status of motherhood. In the remainder of this chapter, we will look at some

THE ULTIMATE WIFE

examples of great biblical mothers.

Hannah, Mother of Samuel

> And Elkanah, her husband, said to her, "Hannah, why do you weep? And why do you not eat? And why is your heart sad? Am I not more to you than ten sons?"
> **9** After they had eaten and drunk in Shiloh, Hannah rose. Now Eli the priest was sitting on the seat beside the doorpost of the temple of the LORD. **10** She was deeply distressed and prayed to the LORD and wept bitterly. **11** And she vowed a vow and said, "O LORD of hosts, if you will indeed look on the affliction of your servant and remember me and not forget your servant, but will give to your servant a son, then I will give him to the LORD all the days of his life, and no razor shall touch his head."
> **12** As she continued praying before the LORD, Eli observed her mouth. **13** Hannah was speaking in her heart; only her lips moved, and her voice was not heard. Therefore Eli took her to be drunk woman. **14** And Eli said to her, "How long will you go on being drunk? Put your wine away from you." **15** But Hannah

THE ULTIMATE WIFE

answered, "No, my lord, I am a woman troubled in spirit. I have drunk neither wine nor strong drink, but I have been pouring out my soul before the LORD. **16** Do not regard your servant as a worthless woman, for all along I have been speaking out of my great anxiety and vexation." **17** Then Eli answered, "Go in peace, and the God of Israel grant your petition that you have made to him." **18** And she said, "Let your servant find favor in your eyes." Then the woman went her way and ate, and her face was no longer sad.

19 They rose early in the morning and worshiped before the LORD; then they went back to their house at Ramah. And Elkanah knew [made love to] Hannah his wife, and the LORD remembered her. **20** And in due time Hannah conceived and bore a son, and she called his name Samuel, for she said, "I have asked for him from the LORD."
(1 Samuel 1:8-20 ESV)

Hannah did not forget her promise to God. She dedicated her son to the Lord, and Samuel grew and he became a great prophet.

THE ULTIMATE WIFE

The man Elkanah and all his house went up to offer to the LORD the yearly sacrifice and to pay his vow. **22** But Hannah did not go up, for she said to her husband, "As soon as the child is weaned, I will bring him, so that he may appear in the presence of the LORD and dwell there forever." **23** Elkanah her husband said to her, "Do what seems best to you; wait until you have weaned him; only, may the LORD establish his word." So the woman remained and nursed her son until she weaned him. **24** And when she had weaned him, she took him up with her, along with a three-year-old bull, an ephah of flour, and a skin of wine, and she brought him to the house of the LORD at Shiloh. And the child was young. **25** Then they slaughtered the bull, and they brought the child to Eli. **26** And she said, "Oh, my lord! As you live, my lord, I am the woman who was standing here in your presence, praying to the LORD. **27** For this child I prayed, and the LORD has granted me my petition that I made to him. **28** Therefore I have lent him to the LORD. As long as he lives, he is lent to the LORD."

And he worshiped the LORD there.
(1 Samuel 1:21-28 ESV)

THE ULTIMATE WIFE

Elizabeth, Mother of John the Baptist

Elizabeth was another godly mother who was blessed with a child after waiting for many years to have a baby:

> After this, his wife Elizabeth became pregnant and for five months remained in seclusion. **25** "The Lord has done this for me," she said. "In these days he has shown his favor and taken away my disgrace among the people."
> (Luke 1:24-25 NIV)

> In a loud voice she exclaimed: "Blessed are you among women, and blessed is the child you will bear! **43** But why am I so favored, that the mother of my Lord should come to me? **44** As soon as the sound of your greeting reached my ears, the baby in my womb leaped for joy. **45** Blessed is she who has believed that the Lord would fulfill his promises to her!"
> (Luke 1:42-45 NIV)

Mary, Mother of Jesus

When the Angel told Mary that she was going to have a baby, she was very happy and accepted the prophecy with whole heart: "'I am the

THE ULTIMATE WIFE

Lord's servant,' Mary answered. 'May your word to me be fulfilled.' Then the angel left her" (Luke 1:38 NIV). She praised God for the news:

"My soul glorifies the Lord
47 and my spirit rejoices in God my Savior,
48 for he has been mindful
of the humble state of his servant.
From now on all generations will call me blessed,
49 for the Mighty One has done great things for me—
holy is his name.
50 His mercy extends to those who fear him,
from generation to generation.
51 He has performed mighty deeds with his arm;
he has scattered those who are proud in their inmost thoughts.
52 He has brought down rulers from their thrones
but has lifted up the humble.
53 He has filled the hungry with good things
but has sent the rich away empty.
54 He has helped his servant Israel,
remembering to be merciful

THE ULTIMATE WIFE

55 to Abraham and his descendants forever, just as he promised our ancestors."
(Luke 1:46-55 NIV)

After the birth of Christ, Mary and Joseph dedicated Jesus to God in a temple as required by Jewish law. The dedication of your children is a meaningful way of expressing your appreciation to God and of asking Him to protect your baby.

When the time came for the purification rites required by the Law of Moses, Joseph and Mary took him to Jerusalem to present him to the Lord **23** (as it is written in the Law of the Lord, "Every firstborn male is to be consecrated to the Lord"), **24** and to offer a sacrifice in keeping with what is said in the Law of the Lord: "a pair of doves or two young pigeons."
(Luke 2:22-24 NIV)

Godly parents always seek to train their children well from the beginning so that the children will grow up to become God-fearing believers. Mary and Joseph ensured that Jesus was raised properly in their faith and attendant traditions. Just because their son was the Son of God didn't mean that they did not have to be active

THE ULTIMATE WIFE

parents and concerned for His spiritual wellbeing. They also experienced anxiety as Jesus grew more independent and sure of His purpose. This is clear from the account of their family trip to Jerusalem for Passover when Jesus was an older child:

> Every year Jesus' parents went to Jerusalem for the Festival of the Passover. **42** When he was twelve years old, they went up to the festival, according to the custom. **43** After the festival was over, while his parents were returning home, the boy Jesus stayed behind in Jerusalem, but they were unaware of it. **44** Thinking he was in their company, they traveled on for a day. Then they began looking for him among their relatives and friends. **45** When they did not find him, they went back to Jerusalem to look for him. **46** After three days they found him in the temple courts, sitting among the teachers, listening to them and asking them questions. **47** Everyone who heard him was amazed at his understanding and his answers. **48** When his parents saw him, they were astonished. His mother said to him, "Son, why have you treated us like this? Your father and I have been anxiously searching for you."

THE ULTIMATE WIFE

49 "Why were you searching for me?" he asked. "Didn't you know I had to be in my Father's house?" **50** But they did not understand what he was saying to them.
51 Then he went down to Nazareth with them and was obedient to them. But his mother treasured all these things in her heart. **52** And Jesus grew in wisdom and stature, and in favor with God and man.
(Luke 2:41-52 NIV)

Jesus loved Mary deeply and, though He bore unconditional love toward all mankind and carried the weight of all human history, He was well aware of how blessed He was in His mother. He therefore instructed the disciples to care for Mary mother when He was about to die on the cross:

When Jesus then saw His mother, and the disciple whom He loved standing nearby, He said to His mother, "Woman, behold, your son!" **27** Then He said to the disciple, "Behold, your mother!" From that hour the disciple took her into his own *household*.
(John 19:26-27 NASB, emphasis in original)

THE ULTIMATE WIFE

Eunice, Mother of Timothy

Paul's companion Timothy serves as an excellent example of the influence that mothers have on the faith and spiritual lives of their children. Timothy's grandmother and his mother were both believers, and they taught him the word of God from his earliest years. Paul wrote to Timothy, "I also remember the genuine faith of your mother Eunice. Your grandmother Lois had the same sort of faith, and I am sure that you have it as well" (2 Timothy 1:5 CEV). By the time Paul met him, therefore, Timothy already possessed knowledge about God and was prepared to learn more.

Paul added this encouragement to Timothy, and to all believers, to cling to the wisdom that is found by faith in Jesus and in Scripture:

> Keep on being faithful to what you were taught and to what you believed. After all, you know who taught you these things. **15** Since childhood, you have known the Holy Scriptures that are able to make you wise enough to have faith in Christ Jesus and be saved.
> (2 Timothy 3:14-15 CEV)

Believing mothers and fathers serve as vessels of such faith-inspired wisdom. God often chooses parents to

THE ULTIMATE WIFE

convey belief in Christ to the youngest among us. You ought to ensure that the mother of your children is prepared to be such a vessel.

CHAPTER SEVEN

She is Mature of Mind

When choosing your dream wife, one thing you should consider is a woman's maturity. Paul advised believers to be mature, writing, "Brothers and sisters, don't be like children in the way you think. Well, be babies when it comes to evil, but be adults in your thinking" (1 Corinthians 14:20 CEB).

Contrary to popular belief, maturity has little to do with age. While to some extent, physical development and years of experience are necessary to the cultivation of wisdom, not everyone learns effectively from experience. People develop unevenly in terms of wisdom, emotional growth, and acceptance of adult responsibility and priorities. Therefore, a woman may be grown up yet immature in her thinking, in which case she likely depends upon friends and parents to make

THE ULTIMATE WIFE

decisions for her.

A Woman, Not a Child

In writing to the Corinthians about adult versus childlike thinking, Paul was referring to the way in which some people process information and approach decision-making in their minds. Children tend to have difficulty understanding deeper thought and assessing complex situations. They tend to take words literally and to make decisions based on what is readily apparent, immediately gratifying, and easy, rather than on what is right and prudent.

If your wife is not sufficiently mature to make decisions for herself, then at best you will find yourself overburdened with decision-making as you have to micromanage your family's affairs with minimal support. At worst, your wife will rely on others for opinions, and your marriage will become an open book to her relatives and friends. Such a wife is easily swayed by the opinions of others, bringing confusion and, possibly, ungodly ideas into your household. Paul wrote about the importance of being able to stand firm in truth and love:

> We must stop acting like children. We must not let deceitful people trick us by their false

THE ULTIMATE WIFE

teachings, which are like wins that toss us around from place to place. **15** Love should always make us tell the truth. Then we will grow in every way and be more like Christ, the head... (Ephesians 4:14-15 CEV)

 An immature wife may have all the good intentions in the world, but her husband cannot trust her. You should marry a lady who knows and understands what it means to be a married woman. She can seek opinions from her parents on certain matters, but she should respect the privacy of your marital relationship and your household affairs.

 Most marriages do not survive because at least one of the partners is too immature. If you want a marriage that will last, you must ensure that both you and your potential spouse understand how marriage is supposed to work; you must share common expectations for the relationship; and you must both possess the wisdom to make sound decisions for your family. Genesis 24:57-60 recounts that when Rachel was about to get married, her family asked her whether or not she was prepared to accompany Abraham's servant and wed Isaac. She agreed to go at once to Isaac, making this adult decision of her own free will, and only then did her family bless her and send her on her way:

THE ULTIMATE WIFE

> They said, "Summon the young woman and let's ask her opinion." **58** They called Rebekah and said to her, "Will you go with this man?"
> She said, "I will go."
> **59** So they sent off their sister Rebekah, her nurse, Abraham's servant, and his men. **60** And they blessed Rebekah, saying to her,
> "May you, our sister, may you become
> thousands of ten thousand;
> may your children possess
> their enemies' cities." (NIV)

Some parents are more interested in relieving themselves of a daughter—or in some cultures, in receiving the bride price—than in the welfare of their daughter. They don't consider whether their daughter is mature and truly ready to enter into a marital relationship. As a man, then, you must be wise and consider both your own preparedness and that of your potential spouse before you ask to make her your wife.

Paul described maturity most memorably in 1 Corinthians 13:11: "When I was a child, I spake as a child, I understood as a child, I thought as a child: but when I became a man, I put away childish things"

THE ULTIMATE WIFE

(KJV). Does your future wife speak, think, understand problems, and make decisions as an adult should? If you are serious about settling down and starting a family, then you should only date or court a mature woman—not a girl or someone who still behaves as a girl does.

Characteristics of a Mature Woman

- She is careful about how she presents herself.
- She is not extravagant.
- She is self-effacing and does not seek attention unduly.
- She doesn't fall in love with social status and wealth.
- She possesses self-confidence.
- She has her own life and identity as a person.
- She is caring and supportive.
- She demonstrates awareness of what is transpiring in her life and others' lives.
- She knows her own needs and wants.
- She is a balanced and gracious giver as well as receiver.
- She does little things to show that she cares.
- She knows how to stand up for her rights and dues when necessary.

THE ULTIMATE WIFE

- She knows when to be quiet and listen.
- She is a team player.
- She can keep secrets when needed.
- She is honest in her communication.
- She knows her own strengths and weakness.
- She has sense of humor, including about herself.
- She understands that no one is perfect.
- She can forgive easily.
- She is not judgmental.
- She doesn't keep records of others' wrongs.
- She doesn't hold onto anger for long.
- She is emotionally balanced.
- She has the ability to sympathize.
- She is not jealous when her husband must talk to other women.
- She recognizes her fears, but fear doesn't rule her life.
- She is not pessimistic.
- She is teachable and always wants to learn more.

Let us conclude this chapter by examining the benefits of maturity in a wife.

A mature woman is inclined toward long-term

THE ULTIMATE WIFE

commitment.

A woman who is mature does not threaten a man with break-up or an end to their relationship over minor issues. Because she is mature and serious about the relationship, she will always provide a chance to resolve disputes, which inevitably arise in a long-term relationship, in a civil and peaceable manner.

A mature woman copes effectively with unconstructive criticism.

One thing that a mature lady can do is to address capably any negative comments that others may make about her, you, your relationship, or your family. Many people are habitual gossips and speak ill of others as a matter of course, but a mature couple will not let the poisonous words of strangers, neighbors, or even relatives to affect their relationship. A mature husband and wife concern themselves with building a strong family that will meet God's approval, not that of thoughtless people with loose tongues. If your wife is a mature woman, then she will receive compliments and criticism alike in stride, not permitting others' words or opinions to sway her or to distort her view of herself. A husband and wife ought to be secure in their identities, their relationship, and their choices.

THE ULTIMATE WIFE

A mature woman makes decisions based on faith, not feelings.

Hebrews 11:1 declares, "Faith makes us sure of what we hope for and gives us proof of what we cannot see" (CEV). A mature woman demonstrates consistency in her decision-making and stability in her relationships because her faith is the basis of all that she does. Her belief enables her to master her emotions, including her fears.

A mature woman expresses appreciation regularly.

Mature women appreciate the small blessings in life. A mature wife will never ask for more than what you can responsibly offer. If your future wife is comfortable expressing appreciation, you will be happier and your children will benefit from her example.

A mature woman prioritizes wisely.

You should not need to instruct your spouse in her every action and decision. If she is a mature woman, then she will possess a firm sense of priorities and always act in the best interests of you, her, and your family. An immature woman, however, is unsure of her priorities and makes misguided choices as a result. You need a companion and partner who makes the choices that you would make, even when you are not present,

THE ULTIMATE WIFE

because you share a common understanding of life. A mature wife is confident and consistent in doing the right thing.

A mature woman seeks others' wisdom when necessary.

A mature woman is, nonetheless, teachable. She does not presume to have all of the answers, nor is she ashamed to seek counsel from you, from other adults who have more experience in a particular type of matter, or—in all cases—from God. The Bible approves of such humility, and James 1:5 instructs believers accordingly: "But anyone who needs wisdom should ask God, whose very nature is to give to everyone without a second thought, without keeping score. Wisdom will certainly be given to those who ask" (CEB).

CHAPTER EIGHT

She is Humble

In Proverbs 31:23, the queen describes the husband of a virtuous wife as "a well-known and respected leader in the city" (CEV). Indeed, a woman ought to respect her husband; and her husband, in turn, should take care to be a man whom his wife can be proud to respect.

This is not to say, however, that a wife's respect is contingent on her husband's worthiness. A virtuous wife is humble, honoring her husband and not disgracing him—even if deserves ridicule. A wife oughtn't insult her husband any more than a husband should degrade his wife. Therefore, ask God to grant you a humble wife.

Even the intelligent and otherwise virtuous woman Abigail insulted her husband behind his back, calling

THE ULTIMATE WIFE

Nabal a "wicked man" and a "fool" in her conversation with David (1 Samuel 25:25). Though these asperations were accurate, the Bible states that wives are, ultimately, to submit to their husbands. Paul says as much, unambiguously, in Ephesians 5:22-24:

> A wife should put her husband first, as she does the Lord. ... **24** Wives should always put their husbands first, as the church puts Christ first. (CEV)

Of course, men are not perfect, as Christ is; yet, generally speaking, a wife is supposed to revere and respect her husband as the leader of the household. To be certain, she is not supposed to disparage her spouse. It was one thing for Abigail, as a prudent woman, to be aware of Nabal's faults; but in a moment of bitterness, fear, or other weakness, she unnecessarily gave voice to her observations and called him an idiot in front of strangers. As it was, Abigail was walking a fine line by going to David behind her husband's back. She did so for honorable reasons—for Nabal's own sake, we can only assume, and for the sake of their family—and she accomplished this without defying her husband directly. However, choosing to rub his name in the dirt was clearly crossing a line.

THE ULTIMATE WIFE

The Danger of Pride

Pride is dangerous; it can easily destroy a marriage and a family. The history of pride originates with Satan himself, for that was the sin that expelled him from heaven, as the book of Isaiah recounts: "How you have fallen from heaven, morning star, son of the dawn! You have been cast down to the earth, you who once laid low the nations" (Isaiah 14:12 NIV).

Satan was not created evil, according to the Bible. God created Satan as a wise and beautiful angel, one of His heavenly children:

"...'Thus says the LORD God:
"You were the signet [seal] of perfection,
full of wisdom and perfect in beauty.
13 You were in Eden, the garden of God;
every precious stone was your covering,
sardius, topaz, and diamond,
beryl, onyx, and jasper,
sapphire, emerald, and carbuncle;
and crafted in gold were your settings
and your engravings.
On the day that you were created
they were prepared.
14 You were an anointed guardian cherub.
I placed you; you were on the holy mountain of

THE ULTIMATE WIFE

God;
in the midst of the stones of fire you walked."
(Ezekiel 28:12-14 ESV)

Then Satan became arrogant in his beauty and status, and he decided he wanted a throne above that of God. Note the frequency of first-person, self-referencing pronouns—evidence of his sinful pride—in these verses:

You said in your heart,
"*I* will ascend to the heavens;
I will raise my throne
above the stars of God;
I will sit enthroned on the mount of assembly,
on the utmost heights of Mount Zaphon.
14 *I* will ascend above the tops of the clouds;
I will make myself like the Most High."
(Isaiah 14:13-14 NIV)

Satan can easily manipulate arrogant people because pride is now the essence of his own character. Pride is the antithesis of humility and the root of all manner of evil; it leaves no space for true love. Not coincidentally, pride is also one of the main causes of separation and divorce. Men and women struggle to humble

THE ULTIMATE WIFE

themselves in their homes. This is something that you must consider when choosing your future wife. You and your spouse must both heed the advice of Peter, who said, "Likewise, you younger people, submit yourselves to *your* elders. Yes, all of *you* be submissive to another, and be clothed with humility, for:

'God resists the proud,
But gives grace to the humble.'"
(1 Peter 5:5 NKJV, emphasis in original)

A number of different factors may lead a woman to act proudly and disrespect her husband as Abigail did. As a man searching for his dream wife, you must consider these factors seriously.

Her Education

Increasingly in modern times, women are highly educated; and because of their education, they find it difficult to submit to husbands who lack much formal education. If your education ended with a high school diploma but you decide to marry a woman with a graduate degree, the relationship may start out well enough. However, as times goes on, this disparity of education almost always creates wrinkles in the marital relationship. It becomes a burden if you find yourselves unable to speak or think about the same things or in the same way. Moreover, the Bible says that a man is to be the head of the family, but a more-educated wife may not trust her husband; rather, because she knows more than he does, she may think that she knows better as well.

I am not suggesting that you discount marriage to a woman who has higher educational qualifications than you do. However, you must be careful, and you should spend sufficient time with her to determine whether the difference is likely to drive a wedge between you in the future. There is a saying, "Cut your coat according to your size, and your coat will fit you perfectly." The closer you are to your spouse in level of education, generally the better.

Her Occupation

It is also important to consider the occupation of the women whom you plan to marry. Some women are engaged in jobs or professions that require them to be strong authority figures and decision-makers. This is only a problem to the extent that it renders a woman unable to humble herself toward their husband. A woman who is accustomed to controlling and commanding other people in the office may prove reluctant to recognize her husband as the chief authority

THE ULTIMATE WIFE

in the home. Without meaning disrespect, she might sometimes forget herself and try to order her husband about as she would an employee.

Therefore, if God leads you to marry a woman who exercises authority in her job outside the home, don't expect that submission to you as her husband will come easily to her. God can change her behavior if her heart is willing, but you must be patient and understand her struggle. If you are a man who hates being instructed, then you might think twice about marrying such a woman in the first place.

Her Family Background

You should consider, too, the previous family life of your future spouse. If a woman hails from a wealthy family, she may find it difficult to humble herself toward her husband, or his family, if they are of a lower class or socio-economic status. If you want to marry a rich lady, you should also prepare yourself for certain assumptions that she will doubtless bring to the marriage. A woman who was born and raised as a princess will not transform readily into a servant. The likely result will be a tug of war over the sharing of household duties and over expectations about the material lifestyle of your family.

In terms of a woman's position within her previous

THE ULTIMATE WIFE

household, an eldest child is more likely to assume an authoritative role while a youngest child may be accustomed to coddling. This is not to say that any woman cannot be your, or someone's, dream wife; but realize that people seldom change overnight.

Her Culture

Culture also complicates the matter of a woman acting humbly toward her husband. This factor is especially common in those countries where men and women are treated as full political and social equals. If you plan to marry a woman from such a country, or live in such a society, then be prepared for that egalitarian sensibility. It is important to understand your future wife's cultural assumptions, as well as to learn more about the country and culture that you are entering if you intend to join her in an unfamiliar place. Such considerations are best investigated before making any final decision about marriage. Though a believing wife should still defer to you in decision-making and spiritual matters, you will otherwise function more as equal partners in the home.

Her Age

Age differences, within reason and subject to considerations of maturity, are not necessarily a

THE ULTIMATE WIFE

problem if you know that a woman is the person God intends for you. First is the question of being able to relate to your spouse on a personal level, which is why you are best advised to find a wife who belongs to the same generation, at least, as you.

Second, age gaps in which the woman is significantly older than the man bring some concern in terms of wifely respect and humility. If a woman cannot help but regard herself as your elder, then she may be inclined to treat you more as a younger brother than a husband. An older woman may not feel the need to listen to your opinion or respect your judgment because she figures that she has seen more of life than you have. She was born before you, which can make humility and submission a challenge. This poses a problem to your marriage if you find yourself unable to exercise authority in your home. When you marry a woman who is older than you, prepare for occasional coaching. While age discrepancies are not insurmountable in marriage, the resulting tensions are difficult to resolve completely.

Her Social Life

There is a saying, "Show me your friends and I will show you your character." While a woman's social circle does not always reflect her level of maturity or other

THE ULTIMATE WIFE

virtues accurately, you can nonetheless gauge the kind of wife you are pursuing by observing her friends. The way her peers speak and behave may serve as a godly influence, if they themselves are virtuous women—or it may encourage her to be disrespectful and unladylike, if they are not. Peer groups' influence cannot help but seep into a person's home life, which is why Paul asked the Corinthian church, "What relationship does light have with darkness?" (2 Corinthians 6:14).

Her Spirituality

You may think that if you marry a deeply spiritual woman, your home life will be peaceful, but sometimes the opposite is true. If you marry a woman whose regards herself as more spiritually mature than you are, she may be inclined to treat you like a baby. If your wife views you as a spiritual infant, then she may not respect you, trust your judgment, or submit to your leadership. Such a woman may know her way around the Bible, but her application of biblical knowledge to her marital life is lacking. Even if an intensely spiritual wife is entirely sincere in her faith and devoted to her husband, she may sometimes be tempted or feel obliged to supersede your authority in the home. I know couples who struggle for no more reason than that the wife is more deeply committed to her walk with God than her

THE ULTIMATE WIFE

husband is.

However, some spiritually invested women go so far as to condemn or otherwise blatantly disrespect their own husbands who are not as active in the church or as experienced and knowledgeable in matters of faith. Such a wife fails to treat her husband well because she expects the man to be in the same place as she is spiritually. Some men even stop attending church because their wives judge them so severely every step of the way.

Marrying a religious or spiritual woman is no guarantee for a successful marriage. She could be a pastor, Sunday school teacher, Bible study leader, music director, worship leader, prayer leader, or Bible college graduate; yet she may struggle to exhibit humility toward you as her husband. Therefore, instead of choosing a spouse based on her spiritual resume or involvement in the church, allow God to lead you in your search for your dream wife.

A Humble and Submissive Wife

The Bible says that women should humble themselves to their husbands no matter what—regardless of education, job, family and cultural background, age, or spirituality. If you choose a humble wife, you will be far more blessed than if you wed an

THE ULTIMATE WIFE

arrogant woman because God hates pride. When you marry, you and your wife become one; so you and your family will not remain unscathed if you join yourself to a proud woman.

In the early days of the church, as nowadays, a woman might be married to a non-Christian. Though it's not advisable to choose a non-believing spouse voluntarily, the situation may arise, especially if a wife becomes a Christian after marriage. However, the apostle Peter pointed out that humility is an important virtue for a woman, regardless of her husband's faith. Peter offered these words of wisdom to all wives:

> If you are a wife, you must put your husband first. Even if he opposes our message, you will win him over by what you do. No one else will have to say anything to him, **2** because he will see how you honor God and live a pure life. **3** Don't depend on things like fancy hairdos or gold jewelry or expensive clothes to make you look beautiful. **4** Be beautiful in your heart by being gentle and quiet. This kind of beauty will last, and God considers it very special.
> **5** Long ago those women who worshiped God and put their hope in him made themselves beautiful by putting their husbands first. **6** For

THE ULTIMATE WIFE

example, Sarah obeyed Abraham and called him her master. You are her true children, if you do right and don't let anything frighten you.
(1 Peter 3:1-6 CEV)

A woman should be sure that the man she marries is someone to whom she is willing to submit, and a man should be gracious in his position of authority. Paul elaborates on how husbands, wives, and all people, especially believers, should treat one other:

> Do nothing out of selfish ambition or vain conceit. Rather, in humility value others above yourselves, 4 not looking to your own interests but each of you to the interests of the others.
> 5 In your relationships with one another, have the same mindset as Christ Jesus:
> 6 Who, being in very nature God,
> did not consider equality with God something to be used to his own advantage;
> 7 rather, he made himself nothing
> by taking the very nature of a servant,
> being made in human likeness.
> 8 And being found in appearance as a man,
> he humbled himself
> by becoming obedient to death—

THE ULTIMATE WIFE

even death on a cross!

9 Therefore God exalted him to the highest place
and gave him the name that is above every name,
10 that at the name of Jesus every knee should bow,
in heaven and on earth and under the earth,
11 and every tongue acknowledge that Jesus Christ is Lord,
to the glory of God the Father.
(Philippians 2:3-11 NIV)

CONCLUSION

The Ultimate Wife, A Woman of Virtue

Perhaps you now find yourself overwhelmed by all of the criteria and considerations that you must weigh as you search for the ultimate wife and make decisions about marriage. You may be asking: Is it even possible to find a woman who fits all of these qualifications?

Queen Bathsheba began her advice to her son on finding a virtuous wife with that same question. Look at how the following biblical translations phrase her question in Proverbs 31:10:

Aramaic Bible in Plain English
> Who finds a *diligent woman*? For she is precious beyond incomparable precious stones.

THE ULTIMATE WIFE

English Standard Version
An *excellent wife* who can find?
She is far more precious than jewels.

Holman Christian Standard Bible
Who can find a *capable wife?*
She is far more precious than jewels.

International Standard Version
Who can find a *capable wife?*
Her value far exceeds the finest jewels.

King James Bible
Who can find a *virtuous woman?* for her price *is* [sic] far above rubies.

New International Version
A wife of *noble character* who can find?
She is worth far more than rubies.

New Living Translation
Who can find a *virtuous and capable wife?*
She is more precious than rubies.

To answer the question, then—yes, finding your dream wife is entirely possible, but it is not easy, which

THE ULTIMATE WIFE

is why you need God's help. Remember that every worthwhile thing is difficult to obtain; but once you succeed, your life will be forever enriched. You will take care to maintain a treasure acquired with such effort, and its value will endure. Marriage to a virtuous woman is no different.

Since God instituted marriage in the first place, it only makes sense that God would help you find and choose the perfect woman to complete your life. If you don't consult God and His word, but instead make the decision on what seems right to you, then you will never be happy. As Proverbs 12:4 explains, "A wife of noble character is her husband's crown, but a disgraceful wife is like decay in his bones" (NIV).

Your Dream Wife Is from God

God knew well that men need women to be their friends, helpers, complements, and companions. Genesis 2:18 recalls, "Then the LORD God said, 'It is not good for the man to be alone; I will make him a helper suitable for him'" (NASB). As the rest of the narrative makes clear, God did indeed create women especially for this purpose, for no other creature would suffice:

> The man gave names to all the cattle, and to the

THE ULTIMATE WIFE

birds of the sky, and to every beast of the field, but for Adam there was not found a helper suitable for him. **21** So the LORD God caused a deep sleep to fall upon the man, and he slept; then He took one of his ribs and closed up the flesh at that place.
(Genesis 20-21 NASB)

Though women were thus made for men, husbands do not have license to lord over their wives in a proud manner. The help of a woman is not a mere convenience—rather, we men clearly needed help! Therefore, God made Eve from Adam to be his partner. Moreover, because God created them from one body, they were perfect complements and united perfectly in one body as husband and wife (Genesis 2:22-24).

You need God to be the foundation of your marriage, too. Psalm 127:1 declares, "Unless the LORD builds the house, the builders labor in vain. Unless the LORD watches over the city, the guards stand watch in vain" (NIV).

Although the Bible acknowledges that we receive a material inheritance from our parents, a man receives his wife directly from God: "Houses and wealth are inherited from parents, but a prudent wife is from the

THE ULTIMATE WIFE

LORD" (Proverbs 19:14 NIV). Pray, then, and ask God to help you in finding and choosing your wife. When Abraham sent his servant to find a wife for Isaac, he relied on God to guide the servant. The servant prayed, and the Lord helped him:

> **12** He said, "LORD, God of my master Abraham, make something good happen for me today and be loyal to my master Abraham. **13** I will stand here by the spring while the daughters of the men of the city come out to draw water. **14** When I say to a young woman, 'Hand me your water jar so I can drink,' and she says to me, 'Drink, and I will give your camels water too,' may she be the one you've selected for your servant Isaac. In this way I will know that you've been loyal to my master." **15** *Even before he finished speaking,* Rebekah—daughter of Bethuel the son of Milcah wife of Nahor, Abraham's brother—was coming out with a water jar on her shoulder. **16** The young woman was very beautiful, old enough to be married, and hadn't known a man intimately. She went down to the spring, filled her water jar, and came back up.
> **17** The servant ran to meet her and said, "Give

THE ULTIMATE WIFE

me a little sip of water from your jar."
18 She said, "Drink, sir." Then she quickly lowered the water jar with her hands and gave him some water to drink. **19** When she finished giving him a drink, she said, "I'll draw some water for your camels too, till they've had enough to drink." **20** She emptied her water jar quickly into the watering trough, ran to the well again to draw water, and drew for all of the camels. **21** The man stood gazing at her, wondering silently if the LORD had made his trip successful or not.
22 As soon as the camels had finished drinking, the man took out a gold ring, weighing a half shekel, and two gold bracelets for her arms, weighing ten shekels. **23** He said, "Please tell me whose daughter you are. Is there room in your father's house for us to spend the night?"
24 She responded, "I'm the daughter of Bethuel, who is the son of Milkah and Nahor." **25** She continued, "We have plenty of straw and feed for the camels, and a place to spend the night."
26 *The man bowed down and praised the LORD:* **27** *"Bless the LORD, God of my master Abraham, who hasn't given up his loyalty and his faithfulness to my master.* The LORD has shown me the way to the

THE ULTIMATE WIFE

household of my master's brother."
28 The young woman ran and told her mother's household everything that had happened. (Genesis 24:12-28 CEB)

Dangers of the Blame Game

Even when you wed a virtuous woman, your marriage is hardly guaranteed to be a smooth experience. We are still human beings, and because of our imperfect, sinful human nature, we sometimes make mistakes and have misunderstandings. However, the good news is that God will grant both of you wisdom and grace to handle any problem prudently and in unconditional love.

Unfortunately, most people nowadays see divorce, not God, as the answer to spousal conflict and marital discord. For such people, divorce is only the beginning of their problems. When the couple has young children, they too will feel the pain—often most keenly. An old African proverb observes that when two elephants fight, the grass suffers.

Although God created Eve explicitly for Adam, he was quick to accuse her when trouble stirred in the Garden of Eden, and she too sought to cast blame elsewhere in turn:

Then the man and his wife heard the sound of

THE ULTIMATE WIFE

the LORD God as he was walking in the garden in the cool of the day, and they hid from the LORD God among the trees of the garden. **9** But the LORD God called to the man, "Where are you?"

10 He answered, "I heard you in the garden, and I was afraid because I was naked; so I hid."

11 And he said, "Who told you that you were naked? Have you eaten from the tree that I commanded you not to eat from?"

12 The man said, "The woman you put here with me—she gave me some fruit from the tree, and I ate it."

13 Then the LORD God said to the woman, "What is this you have done?"

The woman said, "The serpent deceived me, and I ate."

(Genesis 3:8-13 NIV)

Most of the time, we don't accept our faults but, rather, blame each other until we can no longer stand the conflict. Then we part ways. Adam and Eve, however, did not divorce. Instead, they recognized their mistakes, accepted the consequences, and started life over again—together. Though their sin necessarily brought added hardship, God had mercy on them.

THE ULTIMATE WIFE

Even in their moment of shame and vulnerability, He covered their nakedness and helped them carry onward: "The LORD God made garments of skin for Adam and his wife and clothed them" (Genesis 3:21 NIV).

Marry a woman who will love you dearly no matter your missteps and no matter the difficulties you encounter. The ultimate wife is a God-fearing, virtuous woman, and your marriage will result in a family that is happy and enduring. You must likewise commit to her, putting all your heart into your marriage; then God will grant you success. Solomon offers this wisdom to husbands:

> Enjoy life with the woman whom you love all the days of your fleeting life which He has given to you under the sun; for this is your reward in life and in your toil in which you have labored under the sun.
> (Ecclesiastes 9:9 ESV)

May God richly bless you—and your dream wife.

ABOUT THE AUTHOR

RICMOND DONKOR is an evangelist, pastor, teacher, encourager, and motivational speaker who lives in Vancouver. He is the founder of Exposed Truth Evangelistic Ministries. Richmond has been preaching, teaching, training and planting churches in the Phillippines, Honk Kong, China, Thailan, Cambodia, and Malaysia and currently is the associate pastor at the Restored House Chapel Ministries in Vancouver, Canada. He enjoys reading, writing, praying, and singing praise and worship songs.

Other books by Richmond are 3 Steps to Overcome Poverty, The Call With Promise, Failure is not Defeat, and How To Evangelize With Confidence.

Made in the USA
San Bernardino, CA
05 July 2014